Praise for *I Wanna Hold Your Hand*

"The play chronicles the bittersweet connections that are often sparked between strangers at the time of unimaginable tragedy and the fragility of that condition that can also lead to frustrating missed connections. Patterson has created a touching and often humorous journey through the struggles that befall—and mostly strengthen—the lives of those afflicted."

—Travis Michael Holder, *Arts In LA*

"The writing displays Patterson's knack for both poetic and realistic dialogue."

—David C. Nichols, *Los Angeles Times*

"An unexpected triumph... *I Wanna Hold Your Hand* contains so much hope and love and new beginnings and is absolutely comforting. Well-thought out, rooted, artistic writing, capturing the laughable and sometimes dark complexities of human nature."

—Tracey Paleo, *Gia On the Move*

"Patterson's moving play, set mostly in a hospital waiting room, concerns two stroke victims and their families dealing with the capriciousness of personal tragedy... A tender fabric of connections and missed connections."

—Sarah Tuft, *Stage Raw*

"It's full of dynamic characters going through interesting changes, and they say funny and moving things... Powerful enough to make me tear up. I was usually fascinated, gape-mouthed, my default position at an engaging entertainment."

—Jason Rohrer, *Stage and Cinema*

I Wanna Hold Your Hand

Plays by Erik Patterson

Tonseisha

Yellow Flesh / Alabaster Rose

Red Light, Green Light

He Asked For It

Sick

I Wanna Hold Your Hand

One of the Nice Ones

Handjob

Books by Erik Patterson

Pop Prompts: 200 Writing Prompts Inspired by Popular Music

Pop Prompts For Swifties: 99 Writing Prompts

I Wanna Hold Your Hand

by Erik Patterson

Camden High Street Books
2023

I Wanna Hold Your Hand is copyright © 2023 by Erik Patterson

I Wanna Hold Your Hand is published by Camden High Street Books

All rights reserved. Except for brief passages quoted in newspaper, magazine, radio or television reviews, no part of this book may be reproduced in any form or by any means, electronic or mechanical, including photocopying or recording, or by an information storage and retrieval system, without permission in writing from the publisher.

Professionals and amateurs are hereby warned that this material, being fully protected under the Copyright Laws of the United States of America and all other countries of the Berne and Universal Copyright Conventions, is subject to a royalty. All rights, including but not limited to, professional, amateur, recording, motion picture, recitation, lecturing, public reading, radio and television broadcasting, and the rights of translation into foreign languages, are expressly reserved. Particular emphasis is placed on the question of readings and all uses of this book by educational institutions, permission for which must be secured from the publisher: camdenhighstreetbooks@gmail.com.

Performance Licensing and Royalty Payments. Amateur and professional performance rights to this Play are strictly reserved. No amateur or professional production groups or individuals may perform this Play without obtaining advance written permission. Required royalty fees must be paid every time the Play is performed before any audience, whether or not it is presented for profit and whether or not admission is charged. All licensing requests and inquiries concerning amateur and professional performance rights should be addressed to the author at erik@erikpatterson.org.

Print ISBN: 978-1-7379853-7-2
eBook ISBN: 979-8-9878016-4-2

Library of Congress Control Number: 2023902613

First Paperback Edition, March 2023

Copy editing by Sherry Angel
Cover image by Jeremy Goldberg on Unsplash

Printed in the United States of America
Los Angeles, CA
www.erikpatterson.org

Thank you, Uma, for the inspiration.

"Half of what I say is meaningless...
but I say it just to reach you..."

—The Beatles
"Julia"
The White Album

PRODUCTION HISTORY

I Wanna Hold Your Hand had its world premiere at Theatre of NOTE in Los Angeles on August 7, 2014. It was directed by McKerrin Kelly. The scenic design was by William Moore, Jr., the lighting design was by Bosco Flanagan, the sound design was by Cricket Myers, the costume design was by Kara McLeod, the prop design was by Misty Carlisle, the production stage manager was Heidi Marie, and it was produced by David Bickford, Jenny Soo, and Alina Phelan. The cast was:

JULIA	Alina Phelan
PAUL	Nicholas S. Williams
MARY	Judith Ann Levitt
JEAN JOSH	Keston John Kirsten
ADA	Vangsness Phil
FRANK	Ward

The understudy cast was: Alexis DeLaRosa, Debbie Jaffe, Jonathon Lamer, Sarah Lilly, Will McFadden, and Nicole Gabriella Scipione.

SETTING

New York City, the last year or so.

CHARACTERS

JULIA, 30s, an actress. She lives with her husband in Brooklyn.

PAUL, 30s, Julia's older brother, a good son. A teacher. He flew out from Boston to be with his family.

MARY JEAN, 60s, their mother. Recovering from a brain aneurysm, censorless in an almost childlike way.

JOSH, 30s, Julia's husband. Handsome, rugged, also an actor.

ADA, 30s, a book editor, a firecracker. She's engaged to:

FRANK, 30s, recovering from a brain aneurysm and a stroke, suffers from aphasia. Some speech comes out fluidly, effortlessly. Other times, it's a struggle. It's clear the words are in there, somewhere in his head—but as hard as he tries, he can't always get them out. It can be frustrating. Other times, it just is what it is.

NOTES

[Words in brackets] should not be said. Slashes indicate overlapping dialogue. Many of the locations can merely be suggested. Transitions should be quick. Let scenes bleed into each other.

MUSIC NOTE

While scene titles reference songs from *The White Album* by The Beatles, the only time we should hear The Beatles is when Julia and Paul listen to them in Scene 10.

SIDE ONE

TRACK 1:
"Back in the NYC"

A hospital chapel. PAUL sits in front of a pew. He speaks to the audience. Urgent. This is life or death.

PAUL: Hi. Hello, hi. It feels weird talking like this,
but I guess this is how people do it?
So I'll just [start] —

When we were kids,
my sister Julia and I,
we didn't go to church like most of our friends.
Our God was a different kind of God than the one most people believed in.

He lived in the record player,
and He had four names:
John, Paul, George, and Ringo,
depending on my mom's mood. Or my dad's.

They were Beatles freaks. Obviously.
I would say "are,"

but Dad's dead, and Mom's in a coma,
so tenses are tricky.

I teach high school English, I'm acutely aware of these things.
Not that anyone else is. You try to teach grammar to kids, but
words are the last thing they wanna think about.

I'm sorry. I don't know what I was trying to say.
My thoughts don't come out straight.
Like my head's on backwards.

Like:
all of these words
are in boxes
in my head
and I reach into a box
that has the right word
but then
I pull out the wrong one instead and I feel like
a fucking idiot, excuse my language.

Now I remember—the coma thing: my mom.

She's in the other room, the ICU, and like I said, she is—was?—
a Beatles freak, so I gave her my iPod and I put on *Abbey Road*
and I hope she can hear it.

There's this story—
my mom, she says she—it's ridiculous, but—
she says she was there when John Lennon was killed.
This was December 8, 1980.

My mom was friends with this woman Amy who lived at the Dakota Building, which is where John and Yoko lived—that should be a fact everyone knows, but some of my students don't even know who the Beatles are, which boggles the mind and their parents should be shot—but back to my mom—on this particular night, mom was at Amy's place having a "night away from the kids." The two of them say goodnight. Mom leaves the building. And as she's walking down the street...she hears gunshots. She runs the rest of the way to the subway. The next day, she hears the news about John Lennon. And mom realizes: she was fifty feet away when it happened.

My mom totally dines out on this story,
but I never really bought it—I mean, *come on*—
that she would be there
at that exact [moment]???
My name's *Paul* for Christ's sake.
No way she was there coincidentally
when one of the Beatles got shot.
Things like that don't happen in real life.

But mom can get away with a story like that because: she's nice. She's one of those really, really nice people. Not in an annoying way, in more of a—it's like you, you marvel at her—you listen to her talk and think: "How did this woman get through so much life and stay so...nice?" I mean, break some dishes or something. But she's just...[nice]. It's the way she was built. Is built.

The point is, my mom's the kind of person who says she was there when John Lennon got shot, and you believe her 'cause you don't wanna believe this woman could lie to you. That's how she got away with this story for so long, even though she couldn't have been there that night. It's too coincidental, or poetic, or sad. I don't know which word I want.

I have this student, Lolita Johnson, that's her actual name. She says coincidences are the universe's way of being lazy. She probably read that on tumblr but it's the smartest thing any of my students has said lately so I gave her an A. She has a great name, doesn't she? Lolita Johnson. It's an absurd name. There was a kid in my sophomore class last year named Richard Holder. He was suspended for masturbating in the quad. Richard Holder. I am not making this up.

I've been sitting in the ICU with my mom all morning.
Holding her hand.

I told her what happened on *Grey's Anatomy* last night. She's
obsessed. She'll be upset she's missing it. I tried to watch *NCIS*
for her, too, but I couldn't do it.

So they shaved half of my mom's head.
I asked one of the nurses
why they didn't shave the whole thing
and this nurse says:
"She'll want some hair when she wakes up."
And I'm like:
"Do you really think she'll only want half of it?"
I made them shave the rest.
They don't know my mom, *I* know my mom.
She doesn't want half a head of hair.

I told you about my dad, right?
I can't remember what I've said and what I haven't said.
It was this accident, this totally stupid...

...he's crossing the street,
he gets hit by a car, and then boom:
he's gone, just like that.
No goodbye, nothing.
But the weird thing is:
it happened on December 8th.
The anniversary of John Lennon's death.

There's that word again: coincidence.
I wouldn't believe it either, but it happened.

After John got shot, mom was in a daze for months. With dad, it only took a week before she was business as usual. I was living in Boston. I came back home to Brooklyn to take care of Mom, but she was...*fine*. I know everyone mourns in their own way— and I even get her thing with John Lennon. This is gonna sound weird, but whatever: I know where I was when I heard George Harrison was dead. If you asked a hundred people their favorite Beatle, the first 95 are gonna say John or Paul, you'd get one freakazoid who says Ringo, and then four people who say George. I'm a George man. Something about the sitar. But even though I love the guy's music, I'm not gonna go around saying I was in the room with George when he died. Because then I'd be crazy.

Sorry mom but it's crazy. And this talking to God thing? This feels crazy too. I've never understood how you can to talk to someone who doesn't have a face.

But my mom had an aneurysm burst,
and I feel powerless,
and alone,
and I wish I had someone, something—
some man,

some woman,

some ball of energy, anything—

someone bigger than myself to talk to.

I always tell my students to "be more specific." So I'm gonna pray, and I'm gonna give you a face.

He closes his eyes.

John Lennon, if you can hear me, please help my mom? She loves you. She really does. She loves you so much she makes up stories about being there the day you got shot. It's a crazy love, an all-consuming love, and I need it to mean something. Her name's Mary Jean Johnson, she's at St. Luke's Hospital, on 12th Street, the 13th floor, ICU 3. *Mary Jean Johnson.* She needs help, so if you could help her, I'd appreciate it. I don't know who else to ask. Thanks, John. I'll owe you one.

Lights shift.

TRACK 2:
"Greet the Brand New Day"

About two weeks later.

St. Luke's Hospital, NYC. The 13th Floor waiting room, outside ICU 3. No windows, small and confined, white and antiseptic.

Sitting in various chairs, we see: JULIA, knitting. JOSH, working on a crossword puzzle. PAUL, eating lunch.

Another man lies stretched out across three chairs, sleeping. He has a winter coat draped over his head to shield his eyes from the harsh halogen lights.

JOSH: Who composed "Bolero"? Five letters.
JULIA: Ravel.
JOSH: Perfect. R-A-V...?
JULIA: E-L.
JOSH: E-L. Ravel.

ADA enters, flustered. Takes off her coat, scarf, and gloves. She throws them onto a chair, with her purse.

ADA: Where's ICU 3? Do you, any of you [know] —oh my God, Ada, breathe, just breathe. Okay, focus, ICU 3—anyone?
JULIA: Down the hall to the left.
ADA: Do I look okay?

Ada runs a hand through her hair.

JULIA: You look fine.
ADA: This is a fucking nightmare, my God. Thank you, sorry.

She shakes out some sound.

Ahhhhh.

She can't get out any more words. She rushes out, leaving her things.

PAUL: Do you wanna guess?
JULIA: I hate this game. It's an awful game.
PAUL: It passes the time.
JULIA: It's her husband.
PAUL: I don't think so, no—

JULIA: Then who do you—
PAUL: A boyfriend. You don't worry about your hair if it's your husband.
JULIA: Yes you do—
JOSH: I need a five-letter word for a spice, beginning with a "c".
JULIA: Cumin.

(*back to Paul*)

She had a ring, she was wearing a ring.
PAUL: I still don't think they're married. She didn't look married.
JULIA: What's that even mean? She didn't "look married," who looks married—
PAUL: She didn't look haggard.
JULIA: She *did* look haggard—
PAUL: Yeah, but that was hospital-haggard, not married-haggard.
JULIA: Do I look haggard?
PAUL: Completely.
JULIA: Shut up, I'm hospital-haggard too. Right honey?

(*nudging Josh*)

Am I hospital-haggard or married-haggard?
JOSH: Hospital-haggard.
JULIA: Thank you.

(*to Paul*)

See?

PAUL: I think she's engaged, maybe. Not married, just—he's her boyfriend. They're engaged.

JULIA: Her fiancé, then. That's what you're saying?

JOSH: Author of Voyage of the Beagle? Six letters.

PAUL: Darwin.

(*back to Julia*)

Yes, her fiancé.

JULIA: Because of the hair thing.

PAUL: Yeah. And you're sticking with "he's her husband"?

JULIA: Yes.

PAUL: Loser buys sandwiches for the whole waiting room tomorrow.

JOSH: I think it's her mom.

PAUL: No way.

JULIA: Definitely not her mom.

JOSH: Why couldn't it be her mom?

PAUL: You're not here every day. When you're here every day, you can tell these things.

JULIA: I'm sorry, baby: it's not her mom. Hey, did I lock up the house when we left this morning? I don't remember locking it.

PAUL: You locked it.

JULIA: I'm gonna go check on mom. See if her eyes are open.

Julia gets up and exits.

JOSH: "Some like it hot." Six letters. Begins with a "t" and ends with an "e."

PAUL: Tamale.

JOSH: ...thanks.

PAUL: Why do you insist on doing the crossword puzzle? You're so bad at it.

JOSH: Don't be a jerk, I'm good.

PAUL: You're not good.

JOSH: It passes the time.

Julia and Ada both come back in.

JULIA: They closed the room. Nurse switch-over. Mom's awake.

PAUL: She's alert?

JULIA: She squeezed my hand, yeah.

(*to Ada*)

Come in. Make yourself comfortable.

PAUL: Which is impossible, by the way. You'd think they'd make these rooms comfortable for the families. It's messed up. You can't get comfortable.

JULIA: But you can try. Come in.

ADA: I'm okay. I'll just [stand here]—I'm fine. I'm fucking fine. I'm

SO fucking fine.

Ada hovers in the doorway.

JULIA: This is my husband Josh—
JOSH: Hi.
JULIA: —and my brother Paul—he's sort of a doctor—
PAUL: I went through EMT training a dozen years ago, so not really.
JULIA: But he still knows stuff, ask him anything. And that guy asleep on the chairs over there, that's Dennis, his son Mark is in the bed across from our mom.
PAUL: Massive head trauma.
JULIA: And then Dennis's wife Denise—
PAUL: —ridiculous, right? Dennis and Denise?
JULIA: —she's usually here too—
PAUL: She's taking Jeff—their other son—to the airport, he had to go back home—
JULIA: Sad. Oh, this is Ada. She's here for her *fiancé*. Brain aneurysm.
PAUL: ...and I'll have the roasted chicken on whole grain.
JULIA: Shut up. Ada, ignore him.
PAUL: Where was the aneurysm?
ADA: His brain?
PAUL: Right, this is the neuro-ICU, I meant specifically—
ADA: Oh, sorry—this is what they—

> *She's been clutching a scrap of paper.*
> *She unfolds it and reads.*

"Subarachnoid hemorrhage from a ruptured aneurysm of the anterior choroidal artery." I don't know what that means.

PAUL: Same as our mom. How old is he?

ADA: Forty-three.

JULIA: That's young, that's good.

ADA: You're not supposed to propose to someone and then you're on the ground having a seizure and suddenly we're in a hospital talking about aneurysms and you're in a fucking coma. I mean, who does that? That's not how life's supposed to work.

JULIA: Our mom's aneurysm ruptured 15 days ago. She was in a coma for 12 days. Then she woke up three days ago.

ADA: Is she okay, is she...?

JULIA: She seems responsive. She looks at us. It's hard to tell.

PAUL: She can't talk yet because of the trach tubes.

JULIA: What's your fiancé's name?

ADA: Frank.

JULIA: Frank. It's good that you're here for him.

ADA: He just got out of his—I don't remember what it was called. I should have written it down.

PAUL: Ventriculostomy?

ADA: Yeah. That. That's what they said. I don't even know what a ven—that—is. I haven't had time to google.

PAUL: They're gonna throw a lot of that vocabulary at you. Just write it down, then come in here and ask us—

ADA: Thank you—

PAUL: The aneurysm—it burst this morning? Then what they're doing right now is: they're draining the cranial cavity. Which could take a while. But he's in good hands. They've been good with our mom.

JULIA: The doctors always say they don't want to give you false hope, but you have to have hope.

PAUL: And there's this sandwich shop around the corner, it's the best. Get the roasted chicken with everything on it. Speaking of which, Julia—

JULIA: *You just ate.* I'll get you one tomorrow.

ADA: This is so...thank you for being so [kind]...this is surreal. He just...he asked me to marry him this morning. When I woke up, the ring...it was on my pillow. And then, we [made love]...and then this.

Beat.

The door's open again. I'm gonna—

She rushes out.

PAUL: Can I take a turn?

JULIA: Yeah, she's alert. Go.

Paul exits.

JOSH: Nine letters. Begins with an "e." The clue is "zone."

JULIA: Erogenous. Does it fit?

JOSH: Spell it.

JULIA: E-R-O-G-E-N-O-U-S.

JOSH: It fits.

JULIA: I miss you. I hope mom gets better soon so Paul can go back to Boston. It's Valentine's Day. I completely forgot. How sad is that? You forgot too, but it's okay. Nurse Kathy has a stuffed teddy bear on her desk, with a big, red heart. That's when I put two and two together. I've never seen Nurse Kathy smile, how does she have a valentine? But it's nice—I love thinking there's someone for everyone in this smelly, old, messed-up world. Even that awful nurse. It makes me wet.

JOSH: Shhh...Dennis can hear you...

JULIA: He's asleep. I'm sending Paul to a hotel tonight. So we can have the place to ourselves. I miss the dimple in your stomach. I miss your tongue. I even miss your scratchy toes.

JOSH: Say the name of that spice again.

JULIA: Cumin?

JOSH: Say it sexy.

JULIA: *Cumin.*

They kiss as the lights shift.

TRACK 3:

"See How the Other Half Live"

Same waiting room. A few days later. Julia and Paul play cards. Ada paces, on her cell phone. In hushed tones:

ADA: No, mom, no change. Frank is completely the same as he was this morning. That's what I said...No, I'm not whispering because I'm hiding something, let me—

JULIA: Do you have any 8's?

ADA: Let me speak—Mom? Mom?

PAUL: Go fish.

ADA: I'm whispering because I'm in the waiting room and we're not supposed to use our cells in here / not because there's been some sort of change—

PAUL: Do you have any 3's?

JULIA: Damn you, two 3's.

ADA: I told you, he's the same, no change—

PAUL: You are so about to go down.

ADA: That's what I just said—

JULIA: Just ask for another card, get it over with.

ADA: —how many times do I have to say it?

PAUL: Do you have any Jacks?

ADA: Are you even listening to me? Mom? Are you crying?

JULIA: One Jack.

ADA: Stop crying. Oh my God, stop crying, please?

PAUL: Now all I need to win is a King.

ADA: I hate it when you cry.

PAUL: Do you have a King?

ADA: You're making this about you, it's not about you—

JULIA: I hate this game.

ADA: It's about Frank.

PAUL: Well?

ADA: Mom? Mom? Stop it.

JULIA: Yes, I have a King.

ADA: I said, stop it.

PAUL: I win.

JULIA: I want a rematch, I demand a rematch.

Paul shuffles the cards.

ADA: Mom, I'm gonna hang up if you don't stop. I'm serious. Please stop crying. You're gonna make me cry and I don't wanna cry. Mom, I'm hanging up. I'll call you later. Okay? Did you hear me? I'm saying goodbye. Goodbye.

She hangs up.

Sorry about that.

JULIA: We weren't listening.

PAUL: We were. We were definitely listening.

ADA: I told her not to come. There's just so much to focus on with Frank. I know it's a cliché that my mom drives me crazy but she drives me crazy and she's the last person I want to see right now, you know?

JULIA: Our mom's kinda the first person we want to see right now.

ADA: Oh God. I didn't—I wasn't thinking. Of course. Sorry.

JULIA: It's okay.

ADA: It's not even true, what I just said. The thing is, when I told her not to come out here, I didn't think she'd actually listen to me. She never listened to me before. And now I can't take it back because I'm stupid and I'm stubborn. And then Frank's parents are gone. I don't mean they're dead, they just aren't around. Frank doesn't talk to them, I don't know how to find them. So now I'm here alone, and—you didn't ask for my life story. I should shut up. I'm sorry.

PAUL: Do you want to play Go Fish?

JULIA: It's a stupid game.

PAUL: Really stupid.

JULIA: But play. Please.

ADA: Sure. Okay.

She scoots her chair closer to them.

Paul deals out the cards.

Julia, do you have any 5's?

JULIA: I do.

ADA: Paul, do you have any 2's?

PAUL: You're a natural.

ADA: Just lucky. You guys are too. I mean, that you have each other. While you're going through all of this. Julia, do you have any Jacks?

JULIA: Go fish.

ADA: I keep waiting for Dr. O'Neil to walk into this room and say everything's gonna be okay. To tell me Frank's awake.

JULIA: I was with my mom the first time she opened her eyes. I was standing there, talking to her, and she just opened them like it was nothing. Like she was waking up from a nap. Like she couldn't figure out what all the fuss was about. I got so excited, I ran to the nurses station to tell them.

ADA: I like that.

JULIA: Paul, do you have any Kings?

He hands over a King.

ADA: I wanna be with him when he opens his eyes the first time.

PAUL: Talk to him. You never know what'll get through, what he'll hear. I read this article about a guy who was in a coma for 30 years and then he woke up. He said he was aware of everything the whole time. Can you imagine?

ADA: That's awful.

JULIA: Ada, do you have any 9's? I know you have a 9, I can feel it.

ADA: What if Frank's in a coma for 30 years?

JULIA: You can't think like that.

ADA: What if he dies?

PAUL: You can't think like that either.

ADA: He makes maps. He works for the Department of City Planning. He looks at the city and turns it into these precise, intricate grids. Have you ever looked at a map, I mean really looked at one? Not to find out how to get where you're going—but to see where you are?

JULIA: I guess I haven't really.

PAUL: I just let the GPS on my phone tell me where to go.

ADA: It's an amazing thing. How each piece of the city is connected. You can't even see most of the connections. The pipes underground. The electrical wires overhead. But the city, they know how everything works together—how it all fits—because they have these maps. The maps that Frank makes. He sees pockets of data everywhere, the imperfect lines, the little pieces of connectivity. His brain is...beautiful, and I—I just—I hate to think about all the horrible things that might be happening to it.

PAUL: You have to try to stay positive.

ADA: He's a good person. Why can't that mean something?

JULIA: It does. It means a lot. These things are just random.

ADA: Sometimes when I'm sad, he'll give me one of those little oranges from the supermarket. He'll call it my "sad orange." I'm supposed to eat it and pretend I'm giving the orange all my sadness. It's the strangest thing, but it works. Every time. It makes me happy. If he isn't around anymore, who's gonna give me sad oranges?

Beat.

I'm sorry. We were playing cards. I don't have any 9's. Go fish.

Lights shift.

TRACK 4:
"How the Life Goes On"

Same waiting room. A week later.

Ada is alone. She says a prayer to herself, under her breath.

Josh enters with several Venti coffees from Starbucks.

ADA: Oh hey—Josh—

JOSH: Hey. You thirsty?

ADA: Ohmygod, thank you, yes...You haven't been around. Julia said you got cast in a play?

JOSH: At the Public. I just got out of rehearsal. It's grueling.

ADA: Congrats. The Public...that's big time.

JOSH: It's this new Chuck Mee adaptation of *The Tempest*. You know, classical. Half the time I don't know what I'm saying.

ADA: That's rough.

JOSH: It's not a very big part. Stephano. Do you—

ADA: I don't know the play.

JOSH: Shakespeare. Heady stuff. Julia and I met doing a production of *King Lear*, so the Bard's kind of, like, cupid to us. You know: romantic. Is she here?

ADA: Visiting hours are over.

JOSH: But they didn't kick you out?

ADA: I flirted with Nurse Kathy. She's totally gay for me.

JOSH: I didn't know she was gay.

ADA: She's not. It's an expression.

JOSH: Oh. Right.

ADA: We like each other, we get each other.

JOSH: You "get" Nurse Kathy?

ADA: So she let me stay. I'm not in the mood to go home yet tonight. How'd you get back in here after hours?

JOSH: Carlos in the lobby. He's gay for me too. But literally.

ADA: I bet he likes your smile.

JOSH: It's a good smile.

ADA: It's okay.

JOSH: And I got him a Caramel Mocha. Everyone likes a Caramel Mocha.

ADA: You are such a tease.

JOSH: You do what you gotta do.

ADA: Thanks for the coffee. I needed it.

JOSH: So...how's Frank doing?

ADA: No change. No significant change.

JOSH: Sorry.

ADA: Small, infinitesimal changes, sure.

JOSH: Sure.

ADA: But I'm still waiting for the big change.

JOSH: But what does Dr. O'Neil say?

ADA: I haven't seen him all day. There was a moment this morning when I think maybe Frank might have squeezed my hand, but I couldn't really tell for sure.

JOSH: I bet he did. That's a good sign.

ADA: Your mother-in-law, though. Oh my God, she's doing so great.

JOSH: Really great.

ADA: It's amazing. It really is.

JOSH: Julia said she took a turn for the better today.

ADA: Like, leaps and bounds.

JOSH: They're transferring her to the 4th floor in the morning. They might send her home as early as Monday. I mean, she'll have therapy, but—

ADA: But she's going home. That's amazing.

JOSH: And it'll be nice to get my wife back. Just talking to her on the phone, the relief in her voice—I'm sorry, I don't mean to sound happy.

ADA: You should sound happy.

JOSH: But with the condition Frank's in—

ADA: Don't apologize. You guys are fifteen days ahead of me and Frank. I look forward to being in the happy place you're all in right now. I'll see you there in fifteen days.

JOSH: Of course you will.

ADA: Save me a seat.

Over there in the Land of People You Love Getting Healthy.

JOSH: Done.

Oh guess what: I saw Dennis today.

ADA: You did?

JOSH: He was walking out of the sandwich shop as I walked past with my arms full of coffee.

ADA: You heard about his son, right?

JOSH: Julia told me. So sad. How old was he?

ADA: Twenty-one.

JOSH: Dennis said he missed the chicken breast with everything on it. That it felt weird not eating there every day.

ADA: That's what you guys talked about? Sandwiches?

JOSH: We're men.

ADA: But how did he seem?

JOSH: Bad. Obviously. I mean, he can't be good. His son just died.

ADA: But I was hoping, maybe—did he seem "together" at least?

JOSH: He seemed like he was hungry for a sandwich.

ADA: You know what? I don't want to talk about it. I don't want to think about why Dennis and Denise aren't here. Frank might have squeezed my hand today. That's what I need to focus on.

JOSH: Right. Yes. Smart.

ADA: The good things.

Beat.

There's already someone new in Mark's bed. Her name's Sarah something. Her parents don't really speak English so I didn't get much out of them. Big family.

JOSH: That's good. They'll be a good distraction.

ADA: Everyone'll be here at the crack of dawn tomorrow. We'll be fighting for chairs. So weird: as soon as a bed opens up, there's a new sad story to fill it. Just another day in the neuro-ICU. Life goes on, right?

JOSH: What happened to Sarah something?

ADA: Hit by a bus. Traumatic subdural hematoma.

JOSH: That sucks.

They each take a sip of coffee.

Awkward silence.

Ada just nods. Josh grabs an old People magazine off the side table, starts flipping through it. After a beat...

ADA: Hey. Put the magazine down and look at me.
Tell me a secret.
Something juicy you never told anyone.

JOSH: Why?

ADA: 'Cause tomorrow you could get in a car accident, or have a brain aneurysm, or a meteor could destroy the planet, or some other unforeseeable thing. And if you're harboring a dark secret you don't wanna die with, you should let it out. Whatever you say stays in this room. No judgement.

JOSH: Okay.

ADA: Really?

JOSH: Sure. But you've gotta do it too.

ADA: We'll say them at the same time. So no one can chicken out.

JOSH: On the count of three?

ADA: Three...two...one:

JOSH: I was gonna / ask Julia for a divorce the day her mom's head exploded.

ADA: I'm a terrible person.

JOSH: Wait, what? *That* was your secret? You're a "terrible person?"

ADA: You're leaving Julia?

JOSH: Back up, we're not on me, we're on you.

ADA: I'm a terrible person. I've never told anyone that.

JOSH: Don't you think that's more, like, an emotion than a secret?

ADA: I guess. Now that you mention it.

JOSH: Because it's not on par with the secret I told you.

ADA: It's not a contest.

JOSH: Mine was an actual secret. Yours was just self-pity.

ADA: Mine was a brutal fact.

JOSH: You can't tell Julia what I said.

ADA: Cross my heart and hope to die.

JOSH: I'm not gonna do it anymore. Her mom's aneurysm was a blessing. I can't believe I said that. But it stopped me. You can't leave a person the day their mom's aneurysm bursts.

ADA: Unless you're an asshole.

JOSH: Exactly. These last few weeks, they've brought us closer together. The stuff that wasn't working doesn't matter anymore.

ADA: What wasn't working?

JOSH: I don't always...understand her.

ADA: Women are notoriously enigmatic, though, right?

JOSH: It's more like I literally don't get what she's talking about. I just nod and change the subject. It makes me feel like she thinks she's better than me. But she's not, and I'm not leaving her anyway, so it's a mute point.

ADA: It doesn't speak?

JOSH: Please don't tell Julia I said any of that.

ADA: As long as you don't tell anyone I'm a terrible person.

JOSH: Not fair. But fine. Look, I thought Julia would be here. I came straight from rehearsal. I should go. See you around?

ADA: Yeah. See ya.

Josh exits. Ada notices...

You forgot your coffee.

She grabs it and starts to go, but something stops her at the door.

Dr. O'Neil?

Lights shift.

TRACK 5:

"My Honey Pie"

A hospital chapel.

Ada dials a number on her cell phone. Waits a beat while it rings. Listens as the voicemail picks up.

Then:

ADA: Frank, it's me, Ada.
    Hey honey. Hey.

I'm at the hospital right now, in their weird little chapel. I know people are supposed to find solace in here, but the air's on way too high. It's like they want you to find solace but maybe not too *much* solace.

I came in here to pray but I don't know how. I'm leaving this message instead. So when you wake up, you'll know I had faith that you're gonna wake up and listen to this message. That's my prayer for you. My sign of faith. Don't laugh! I know you're listening to this in the future, laughing at the thought of your meat-loving, athiest, godless girlfriend saying a prayer, but I honestly don't know what else to do. So fucking stop laughing, okay? No, wait, don't stop. I like that you're laughing. I've missed that laugh, keep doing it. You can laugh at me and my voicemail prayer forever.

There are so many things I want to tell you. I keep having these moments where I'm like: this is so weird. And that's when I'd normally check in with you to see if you find this place as fucking weird as I do. We'd share a look that only you and I understand, and then we'd revel in the weirdness because at least we get to experience the weirdness together. Your coma's getting in the way of our inside jokes.

I hope you can't see yourself right now. Like in those movies when the person's in a coma but their soul's floating above their body having an existential do-I-stay-or-do-I-go crisis? Okay, first of all, if you're having that debate, the answer is YES, YOU STAY. And second, if you're floating around this hospital, try not to get a good look at your body because you look TERRIBLE. Really bad. You have all these tubes coming out of everywhere, and it's upsetting. So don't look.

Sometimes I see your eyes moving back and forth under the lids and I wonder if it's possible for you to dream while you're like this? Can you? Stop listening to this message for one second and look at me right now and tell me the answer to that question.

Okay, a few things you should know about me while you were in your coma:

I'm scared.
Really, really scared.
That's the main thing you need to know.
It's the headline everything else falls underneath.

My biggest fear is that you're going to die.
My second biggest fear is you'll wake up and you won't remember me.
Don't do either of those things, okay?
Promise to come back to me?
If you're listening to this message—sorry, no, when you listen to this message—that means you came back, so thank you for that.

I just talked to Dr. O'Neil.
I need you to know what he said.
Because I need you to help me get past this moment.
I need you to help me be strong again.

We're standing outside the waiting room. He says he has news. I ask: "Is Frank okay?" He says: "No." "Has something changed?" I ask. "I've been waiting for a change. Did he open his eyes? Is he awake?" He says: "I'm sorry, Ada." I say: "Don't be sorry. Tell me you've finished draining the excess blood from his cranial cavity." Because that's how I talk now. The Me from nine days ago wouldn't recognize the Me from today.

He looks at the floor. Like he doesn't know how to say it. And I want to scream at him: "YOU'RE A DOCTOR. SAY IT." But I don't scream. I wait for him to look at me again, to look me in the eyes, and then, politely and calmly, I ask: "Was it a good change or a bad change?" And he says: "It's not good, Ada." He says: "It's not good."

So that's where I am. I'm in the middle of the "not good." I need you to wake up and listen to this message so I can be in the "good" again. Please do that, Frank. I need you to wake up.

She hangs up.

Lights shift.

TRACK 6:

"The Continuing Story Of...Frank"

Starbucks. About eight months later.

Julia puts sugar in her coffee. A man stands next to her, also sugaring his coffee. His right arm is in a brace. He has a slight limp, also on the right. This is FRANK. Julia glances at him.

JULIA: Oh my God.

He looks at her funny.

I know you. Oh my God, you were...you're—

He smiles, awkward.

FRANK: Uh...
JULIA: I forget your name, it's—
FRANK: Frank.
JULIA: Right, you're Frank. I'm Julia.
FRANK: I don't...uh...I don't...

(*struggling for the words*)

...know you.

JULIA: Of course. You wouldn't. Sorry. We haven't actually met. You were at St. Luke's. My mom was in the ICU with you, ICU 3.

FRANK: Sorry, I don't, I don't, I don't know. I don't...remember... this was...the aneurysm.

JULIA: You were in a coma, you shouldn't remember me. Of course, sorry. I don't mean to freak you out, this is—

FRANK: This is weird.

JULIA: Yeah, it is, totally. Sorry. But oh my God you look so good. You're...wow. Is Ada, is she—

FRANK: I love her.

JULIA: I bet. So you're still...[together]? Of course you are, yeah. Of course. Wow. You look so...you look so good.

FRANK: Your...your...how's...your...uh...

JULIA: It's okay, take your time...

FRANK: I'm sorry, it's the aneurysm. Your, how's your, your dad?

JULIA: He's, uh—

FRANK: No, I mean—not your dad, your dad. He—not your dad, your...you know, your—

JULIA: You mean my mom?

FRANK: Yes, your...

JULIA: Mom.

FRANK (*watching her lips*): Mom.

JULIA: Yeah—mom.

FRANK/JULIA (*they say it together*): Mom.

JULIA: Right.

FRANK: How is he?

JULIA: *She*...she's good, thanks. It's been tough. She's living with me, but she's actually doing great. She's walking and talking and everything, no problems, like she's totally normal again. I'm sorry, I didn't mean—to imply—that you're not normal. It feels like a miracle to bump into you like this, to see you standing there, after everything. To think, that the last time I saw you, when they transferred my mom...you hadn't even opened your eyes yet, and here [you are]...it's just amazing. I'm amazed.

FRANK: It's...amazing.

JULIA: I emailed Ada a couple of times, but it's hard to keep in touch. Josh—that's my husband—I think the whole thing's starting to get to him, the loss of privacy, the full house—mom's in the guest room, she's doing great but she still needs someone, she can't live alone—and my brother—you wouldn't remember him either I guess—

FRANK: No.

JULIA: Right, well, he quit his job and moved out here to help with mom. Which is great, but he's on the couch in the living room, and honestly he doesn't help all that much and we have a really small place and sometimes I want to be able to breathe without seeing someone I'm related to. Oh my God why am I burdening you with all of this? I'm sorry: you're a miracle, and I should go. It was good to officially meet you.

She starts to go.

FRANK: Wait. You...

JULIA: ...yeah?

FRANK: You're a miracle...too.

She smiles. Deeply touched.

JULIA: Thank you.

Lights shift.

TRACK 7:
"I Don't Know How You Were Diverted"

Later that night. A kitchen. Julia and Josh make a salad. Paul sits at the table, doing a crossword puzzle.

JULIA: It was heartbreaking, the way he said it.

PAUL: "You're a miracle too."

JULIA: When he's been through so much—

PAUL: That's kind of beautiful.

JOSH: I still can't believe you bumped into him. It seems so...Charles Dickens or something.

JULIA: You read one book and suddenly everything's Dickensian.

PAUL: Seven Down should be "SQUID," not "WHALE," and both of these Across answers are wrong too.

JOSH: You're doing my crossword?

JULIA: Actually, what's shocking to me is that it took *this long* for it to happen. I mean, we live seven blocks away from each other. How have we not bumped into each other sooner?

JOSH: I saw Ada at the market once.

JULIA: When?

JOSH: About a month ago.

JULIA: Why didn't you tell me?

JOSH: It never came up.

JULIA: Was she with Frank? Did you talk to her?

JOSH: No. And no. She didn't see me.

JULIA: Then why didn't you go up to her?

JOSH: I was shopping.

PAUL: I've seen her too. I saw her at Boat Bar. Last Friday night. But I didn't talk to her either.

JULIA: What is wrong with you people?

PAUL: I was afraid she'd tell me Frank was dead. I figured it was better to live with the idea in my head that he was getting better, like mom, than know for certain otherwise.

JULIA: Okay, as messed up as that is, I get that.

JOSH: Wait, his excuse is way more messed up than mine. I was shopping, I was busy—it's socially acceptable to ignore someone when you're shopping. But to ignore them because you're afraid their fiancé's dead and you don't want confirmation? That's a whole other level of messed up.

JULIA: No, it makes sense.

JOSH: You two are the most morbist people I've ever met.

PAUL: Did you say "morbist"?

JOSH: Yeah.

PAUL: That's not even a word.

JULIA: You know, I was thinking...

PAUL: You mean "morbid."

JULIA: We should invite Frank and Ada over for dinner.

PAUL: That's a great idea.

JOSH: No—bad idea, weird idea.

JULIA: What's weird about it?

JOSH: You don't even know them.

JULIA: We have the waiting room thing.

JOSH: You always talk about it like that, the waiting room, but I don't understand how it's a "thing," how that really connects you with a person. It's just a room, it's just a place—

PAUL: You weren't there every day—

JOSH: No, I'm not asking you, I'm asking Julia—

JULIA: Paul's right, you don't know what it was like—

JOSH: As if I was supposed to be there—every day. As if—

JULIA: It was my mom, Josh. She was dying—

JOSH: She didn't die.

JULIA: But we thought she would, we didn't know, we—

JOSH: I was there with you—

JULIA: You went back to work, I was alone—

JOSH: It was a good gig! I thought you were / happy for me.

JULIA: It was a dumb play! And I *was* happy for you. But you disappeared.

JOSH: I had rehearsal, I couldn't be at the hospital twenty-four-seven, but you had your brother, he was there with you—

JULIA: You could have made more time.

JOSH: I can't believe we're doing this again. It's been, what, almost a year? You gonna hold this over my head forever?

JULIA: Maybe.

JOSH: You are so, so, so—

JULIA: What? What am I? Am I "morbist?"

JOSH: You're being completely crazy again.

JULIA: If you don't want to have dinner with Frank and Ada because you think it's too "weird," —then just say so.

JOSH: Why do you always—you're picking a fight, / you're—

JULIA: I am not picking a fight.

JOSH: Whatever, you all have "the waiting room thing," so invite them to dinner.

JULIA: I already did. They're coming over Friday night.

JOSH: Great.

(*noticing at the door*)

Your mom—

JULIA: And my mom—she'll be there too.

JOSH: No, Julia, your mom—

JULIA: It'll be good for her and Frank to meet each other—

JOSH: No, she's—

> *He motions towards the door, where we see MARY JEAN, in a blouse and panties.*

JULIA: Oh my God—

PAUL: Come on, mom, please—

JULIA: Put some clothes on.

MARY JEAN: Nothing nobody hasn't seen before.

JOSH: I'm gonna go out for a bit.

JULIA: Where are you going?

JOSH: I don't know.

MARY JEAN: Let him go, he's not smart enough for you anyway.

PAUL: Wow.

JULIA: *Mom.*

MARY JEAN: What?

JOSH: She's probably right. I'll be back later.

He exits.

JULIA: Are you trying to destroy my marriage?

MARY JEAN: I think you're doing a pretty good job of that yourself.

JULIA: You could at least wear pants around the house.

MARY JEAN: It's hot.

PAUL: I'll get her something to wear, hold on.

Paul exits.

MARY JEAN: I really don't see why this is an issue.

JULIA: Mom, it's common decency—

MARY JEAN: I should be able to dress how I want around my own home—

JULIA: But this isn't your own home. It's my home, / mom—

MARY JEAN: I don't see the difference.

JULIA: My home, my rules.

MARY JEAN: But I'm living here now, so it really belongs to both of us, and honestly, I don't see why you're so upset—

JULIA: You're practically naked—

MARY JEAN: —by the human body. It's just a vagina.

JULIA: Oh my God.

MARY JEAN: It's just a pussy. Are you so afraid of that word? Pussy.

JULIA: Please, mom—

MARY JEAN: And I shaved, so it's pretty. Ease up a little. I didn't raise you to be a Pollyanna. Pussy. You're a pussy, I'm a pussy, everyone's a pussy.

JULIA: This is a nightmare.

MARY JEAN: What are you making, is that a salad?

JULIA: You can have it.

MARY JEAN: You're not going to eat with me?

JULIA: I'm not hungry anymore. I'm going out.

MARY JEAN: Why would you go after him when he ran out like that?

JULIA: Don't talk about my husband like he's the plague.

MARY JEAN: You know I never liked him...

JULIA: No, mom, I didn't know that, before [the aneurysm]...so just shut up? I'm not in the mood. Eat. I'll see you later.

Julia exits.

Mary Jean grabs the salad, starts picking at it. She has a pronounced limp in her right leg. Paul comes back in.

PAUL: I brought you pants.

MARY JEAN: Put 'em on the chair. Sit with your mom?

He sits with her. They eat.

PAUL: Hey, have you—

MARY JEAN: I was enjoying the silence.

PAUL: Mom, come on. I was gonna ask if you took your meds today?

MARY JEAN: This morning.

PAUL: Not tonight?

MARY JEAN: I haven't eaten yet.

PAUL: You were supposed to take them an hour ago.

MARY JEAN: Don't tell me what to do. I take them after I eat.

PAUL: Then...eat.

MARY JEAN: Look at me, I'm eating.

PAUL: I'm getting your pills.

Paul exits.

Mary Jean gets up, dumps the salad from her plate into the trash.

Paul comes back in, catches her.

What are you doing?

MARY JEAN: I don't like salad.

PAUL: There's leftover Chinese. Or I could make you a grilled cheese. What do you feel like?

MARY JEAN: I don't feel like anything.

PAUL: Come on, tell me: what do you feel like?

He grabs her arm.

MARY JEAN: What are you doing, why are you grabbing me?

PAUL: Don't you remember? The thing we used to do. It was, like, our inside joke thing.

MARY JEAN: What thing? Let go of me.

He lets go of her arm.

PAUL: Sorry. You have to take these pills.

MARY JEAN: Give 'em.

He drops a few pills into her palm.

PAUL: Take them now.

MARY JEAN: Yes, sir.

She swallows the pills. He grabs a gallon of ice cream and two spoons.

For me?

PAUL: You have to eat something.

Paul suddenly starts to cry.

MARY JEAN: What are you doing?

PAUL: I'm fine, I'm fine—

MARY JEAN: What's wrong, did you hurt yourself?

PAUL: Nothing, nothing's wrong. I'm just emotional, that's all.

MARY JEAN: What is that? What do you mean you're "emotional"?

PAUL: I'm full of emotion.

MARY JEAN: You're like a woman.

PAUL: I'm just happy you're alive. I'm sorry. I'm done.

MARY JEAN: Why don't you get out of here?

PAUL: Where do you want me to go?

MARY JEAN: Go out and meet someone.

PAUL: I don't want to go out.

MARY JEAN: Hanging out here with your mom all the time?

PAUL: What's wrong with that?

MARY JEAN: Don't be that guy. Go meet someone. Get laid.

PAUL: I'm fine. Thanks.

MARY JEAN: Do we have any whipped cream?

PAUL: No.

MARY JEAN: Whipped cream reminds me of your father.

PAUL: Gross, mom, I don't even want to know what that means—

MARY JEAN: Are you dating someone in Boston you're not telling me about?

PAUL: No.

MARY JEAN: One day, you're gonna make me happy.

PAUL: Are you done with your ice cream?

>*She pushes her empty bowl towards him.*

Then would you please—*please*—put your pants on?

>*Lights shift.*

TRACK 8:
"She's Not a Boy Who Misses Much"

Julia and Josh's living room.

Ada, Frank, and Mary Jean sit together on the couch. Julia, Josh, and Paul are on folding chairs.

ADA: That was such a great dinner, Julia.
JULIA: Oh, I didn't—
JOSH: I'm the cook.
MARY JEAN: One thing he's good at.
JOSH: One thing, that's it. It's the only one. Just the one thing.
JULIA: You guys, be nice.

(*to Ada and Frank*)

They like to bicker.
JOSH: We love it. It's one of our favorite things. Right, Mom?
MARY JEAN: Don't call me that. I am not your mother, thank God.
JOSH: See? And we're so good at it.
ADA: Well, the food was really wonderful, whoever made it. Thank you for having us over.
FRANK: Yes, thank you.
JULIA: I'm sorry we didn't do it sooner.

PAUL: Does anyone want more wine?

ADA: I'd love another glass.

JOSH: I'm gonna get another beer. Anyone need anything from the kitchen? Frank, do you want another beer?

FRANK: Yes.

ADA: Actually he's fine.

FRANK: Yes...please.

ADA: You don't need any more.

FRANK: *You're* drinking.

MARY JEAN: Pauly, baby, come refill your mother's glass.

FRANK: I...want.

ADA: Frank. I'm serious. You don't need any more.

FRANK: You don't stop. Stop. I want it.

ADA (*to Josh*): He's had three. He doesn't need any more. He isn't supposed to have so much with his medication.

PAUL: Oh, is he on Keppra? Klonopin?

ADA: Keppra.

PAUL: That's what our mom's on.

FRANK: —*I want*—

ADA: Well, he's on several.

FRANK: —I want—

PAUL: Right, of course.

> *They aren't even listening to Frank. He bangs his fist on the table.*

FRANK: BEER. Please.

ADA: Fine. Josh, he wants a beer, get him a beer.

Josh exits to the kitchen.

MARY JEAN: I got a new skin cream today. Can you tell? I'm practically glowing. And my skin is so soft. Don't you just love it, Frank? Feel my skin.

FRANK: What?

MARY JEAN: Come on, feel it.

She grabs Frank's hand. Puts it up to her neck.

JULIA: Mom, that's weird.

MARY JEAN: Don't I feel so smooth? Well don't I? Say something.

FRANK: Yes.

MARY JEAN: You're handsome, Frank. Do you know how handsome you are?

FRANK: ...yes.

PAUL (*to Ada*): Don't worry, our mom hits on everyone. It's what she does.

ADA: I'm not worried.

MARY JEAN: I can't believe I was shacked up in a room with you and I didn't get to enjoy it. You're such a man, a man's man, so manly.

FRANK: Thank you?

>*Josh comes back in with two beers. He gives one to Frank.*

MARY JEAN: So what do you remember? From the ICU. Do you remember me?
JULIA: Oh yes—good—this is what I was hoping would happen, I was hoping the two of you would talk about the hospital. What it was like for both of you. Compare notes.
MARY JEAN: How long was your coma? Mine was twelve days. Of course I don't remember a thing about it. Twelve-day nap and here I am. I'm like Sleeping Beauty.
JOSH: You couldn't hear us talking to you at all?
MARY JEAN: I'm bonding with Frank right now, Josh.
JOSH: Because Paul thought maybe you could hear us.
PAUL: It was just something I read.
MARY JEAN: Frank, how long was your coma?
FRANK: I don't — [remember] —

>*He looks to Ada for some help.*

ADA: He opened his eyes on day seventeen.
MARY JEAN: Do you ever wonder what they did to us while we were asleep? I have fantasies of a handsome doctor taking advantage of me. I have the most intense orgasms thinking about it.

JULIA: Okay, mom, that's enough, some thoughts are inside thoughts.

MARY JEAN: That's my cue to shut up. If you lovely people will excuse me, I'll be sitting here like a silent idiot.

She focuses on eating, dramatically.

PAUL: So, Frank, how's the therapy going?

JULIA: Yes, your speech therapy, I meant to ask.

FRANK: It's...

JULIA: Do you go every day?

FRANK: It's therapy. It's just...therapy.

ADA: The therapist comes to our apartment. Three days a week. That's all we can afford right now.

FRANK: It's about...the point is...what's the word again?

ADA: Repetition.

FRANK: Repe...

ADA: Repe-*tition*.

FRANK: ...tition.

JOSH: It sounds like a full-time job.

FRANK (*duh*): Yeah.

JOSH: It's the same with acting. When I'm memorizing lines, I have to go over it and over it and over it. But the brain's amazing because when you really want something to stick, you can make it stick. If you try hard enough, you know?

FRANK: I'm not acting, it's...real life.

JOSH: I know, but I get what you're going through, the repetition thing speaks to me. As an actor. That's what I'm saying.

Frank rolls his eyes. Barely hiding his contempt at the comparison.

PAUL: We should have some sort of benefit for you guys. Raise some money for Frank's therapy.
ADA: That's a really nice thought.
JULIA: It's a great idea.
ADA: But you have your own expenses with your mom, so we couldn't accept that kind of generosity.
FRANK: Yeah, no, I don't [want any more charity]...I don't...It's [a nice thought]...it's, it's—

Beat.

I don't know how to say it.
JULIA: What are you trying to say?
FRANK: I don't...uh, it's...A, B, C, D—no.
PAUL: It starts with a D?
FRANK: I don't want— [charity] —
JOSH: Something you don't want that starts with a "D"?
FRANK: Yes—I mean, no—I mean—
MARY JEAN: Ooo, can I play? Can I speak? I wanna play.
JOSH (*sounding it out*): D-d-d-d...what starts with a "D"?

MARY JEAN: Dingo. Doctor. Dick. Danger.

JULIA: Mom, that's not helping.

ADA: I don't think it starts with a "D" —can you start over? A, B, C, D, E, F...?

FRANK: A, B, C, D, E, F—no.

JOSH: Friends...friendship...fuhhhh, fuhhh, fah, fuh—

MARY JEAN: Fuck!

PAUL: Mom, seriously, stop.

FRANK: It's not, uh...

ADA: You can say it. Just relax, just—it'll come to you.

FRANK: A, B, C—cee.

JOSH: It starts with a C?

MARY JEAN: Cranial. Carrot. Caligraphy. Clarity. Cheese. Condom. Crack. Coconut.

JULIA: Mom, muzzle, put it back on.

ADA: He means "*charity*."

PAUL: Wait, you got it?

ADA: He doesn't want charity.

JULIA: Is that right?

PAUL: Oh, we don't have to do a benefit, it was just a thought—

JULIA: Is that what you were trying to say?

> *It is, but he's frustrated by the guessing game. He just shakes his head.*

FRANK: Never mind.

54

JULIA: Are you sure?

FRANK: Yeah, never mind. I'm...aneurysm.

JULIA: I know, I'm sorry.

FRANK: It's hard. All of this...talking, the people. And her—

(*nodding at Mary Jean*)

She's not me.

JULIA: What do you mean?

FRANK: I mean...I'm not...her.

JULIA: I'm not sure what—are you trying to say that you—

FRANK: Actually, can I go?

ADA: He means the bathroom. It's down the hall, Frank.

FRANK: No. Can I...go home?

JOSH: You're leaving? But I made a crème brûlée.

JULIA: Did I say something wrong?

ADA: I think he's embarrassed he can't talk as well as your mom. I told him they both had the same aneurysm. That he was twelve days behind her. But I think he assumed she'd have aphasia. Maybe I assumed it too. I wasn't thinking. Don't worry, he's okay. It's just not what he expected. Right, honey?

Frank just looks away, hurt.

It's okay. He'll be okay.

JOSH: I should make a toast.

JULIA: I'm not sure if that's— [appropriate]. What are you going to say?

JOSH: I don't know, that's kind of the point of the toast. It just comes out.

PAUL: I think it's a great idea. Toast! Take it away.

FRANK: Can I have more [beer]?

He holds out his empty beer bottle.

JOSH: Oh, you want another?

ADA: Thank you, Josh, but he's had enough.

FRANK: I need—for...[the] toast.

PAUL: I can run into the kitchen—

JULIA: Paul, he's not supposed to have any more.

PAUL: He's an adult. We have more—

ADA: Toast with my water.

FRANK: No.

ADA: Frank, just—take it.

She hands him her water. He takes it.

Josh stands. He holds out his glass.

JOSH: I look around this room at each of you, and...I'm not gonna lie: sometimes I feel like I'm an outsider, maybe that's the actor in me, I'm always on the outside looking in...but my point is, we're fuckin' warriors, you know? Like, life is a war and we've been on the front lines and now we have battle scars. Especially you, Mary Jean. Your battle scars are on your head, literally. Which is so intense. And I know we have our differences, but...sometimes I picture you in your coma and then I look at you now and I'm like whoa. I'm just like WHOA. And you, Frank. What you're going through. I mean: wow. Just...wow. Anyway, this—this is for you guys.

> *They improvise various cheers ("For Frank!" "For Mom!") as they toast.*

Now I think I'll go torch the brûlée.
JULIA: Good idea.

> *Josh exits to the kitchen. Julia starts collecting plates. Paul helps her.*

MARY JEAN: It's the other thing he's good at. My son-in-law the pastry chef. Oh, excuse me, am I still not supposed to speak?
JULIA: Mom.
MARY JEAN: I forgot I was wearing a muzzle.
FRANK: Maybe I should be dead.
JULIA: What?
FRANK: Maybe I should be dead. Maybe I should. Maybe I should. I should. Maybe?

ADA: Why would you say that?

FRANK: Maybe I should. I can't be...her. I can't...speak. I can't talk. I can't...speak. I can't... Maybe I should, it would be easier if I was [dead]...maybe that's what I should be?

ADA: Okay, we're gonna go, he's had too much to drink. This is what I was talking about.

FRANK: I can't...read. I can't...write. I can't, I can't.

JULIA: Those things are gonna come back, Frank.

FRANK: Will they?

JULIA: You're working hard and as long as you keep working hard, those things—your speech...it's gonna get better.

FRANK: Is it, though? Is it? Be real.

JULIA: I believe that it will. We're both miracles, remember? You're standing here. If you don't give up, it has to get better.

FRANK: But is your...your dad...is he better?

PAUL: Our dad's dead.

JULIA: He means mom.

FRANK: Yeah, is he, is she...better?

MARY JEAN: I'm better.

FRANK: No. No.

    Be real.

    You be real with me.

    You're all fake.

    You're all...um, uh.

    It's hard and it's awful and it's not happy, nice dinners.

    Look at me.

What is this?
Why are we here?
This is...all I am...now.
I want my old job back.
But, but, but—
the lines don't make sense.
The grids, I get frustrated.
There are so many things I want to do,
all these things I want to say,
it's in my head,
it's all in there—
here, in here—
[but] I can't get it out.
I don't, uh, uh, I don't.
I want, I, I, I want...
Excuse me, I'm sorry, I'm rushing.
Sometimes I have to breathe.
What I'm trying to say.
I'm—

(*a calming breath*)

I want to go back.
Before the aneurysm.
Before, before, before [I knew] any of you.
Before I knew you.

Just Ada.

She's the only part of

any of this

I still want.

Can you send me back?

Send me back.

Please.

Beat. No one has any answers, no one knows what to say.

Josh re-enters, with dessert.

JOSH: And the crème brûlée is served.

Lights shift.

END OF SIDE ONE: INTERMISSION

SIDE TWO

TRACK 9:
"Frank My Dear"

The next night. A hotel room. Ada and Josh are in bed, naked.

ADA: That was so fucking good.
JOSH: I aim to please.
ADA: I don't usually sleep with other people's husbands.
JOSH: Me neither.
ADA: Funny.

Beat.

I don't think of you as "Julia's husband." You weren't at the hospital very much—
JOSH: You're gonna give me grief about that too?
ADA: —so I never had a very clear picture of the two of you together. Then seeing you with her at dinner last night...
JOSH: I should've left her when I was gonna leave her. While her mom was in the hospital. I realize that now.
ADA: I know you say that, but—
JOSH: You're not a homewrecker.
ADA: Well...

JOSH: You're not.

ADA: But seeing the two of you together, the "couple" part of you suddenly made sense. The "you and Julia" part of you. It made me feel bad calling you today.

JOSH: Good bad? Or dirty bad?

ADA: No, just...bad. Plain bad.

JOSH: Oh. Well, don't.

ADA: I don't want to hurt Julia. I like her.

JOSH: Me too, I do too.

Beat.

ADA: You have a pimple on your shoulder.

JOSH: Where?

ADA: Right there. Can I...[pop it]?

JOSH: Sure.

She reaches over, squeezes the zit.

Ow, not too hard!

ADA: Sorry.

Beat.

Julia's mom seems...I don't know how to finish that sentence.

JOSH: She's okay. She's kind of a bitch.

ADA: I've never heard a mother use the word orgasm before—I mean, good for her for having them, but—

JOSH: All of that's new, the sex stuff.

ADA: So she didn't used to be such a horny bastard?

JOSH: She doesn't censor anymore. She says what she's gonna say. And a lot of the time it's about sex. It's awkward.

ADA: I think it's great. When I'm 60, I wanna be having as many orgasms as possible, you know?

JOSH: Just don't tell your kids about it.

ADA: Oh, I'm not having kids. The world's too messed up.

JOSH: What about Frank? Is he—

ADA: He doesn't want kids either.

JOSH: No, I mean—

ADA: Is he different?

JOSH: Yeah.

ADA: He's the same.

JOSH: But does he—

ADA: Please. Stop. Stop it with the Frank stuff.

JOSH: Oh, sorry—

ADA: I don't want to talk about him, so just shut up, okay?

JOSH: Okay. Sorry.

Josh checks his cell phone.

ADA: Anyway.
JOSH: So...

ADA: God, I'm sorry, I shouldn't have told you to shut up.

JOSH: It's okay.

ADA: I'm worse than your mother-in-law. I'm the bitch.

JOSH: You're not a bitch.

ADA: I am, and you're just gonna have to deal with it if we're gonna do this.

JOSH: You still wanna do this?

ADA: Yeah. Sure.

>*Nice. Josh puts the cell phone down.*

JOSH: Because if you want another orgasm right now...

ADA: Really?

JOSH: I definitely have another one in the chamber.

ADA: I would be okay with that.

JOSH: Yeah?

ADA: Yeah. Let's get kinky.

>*She kisses him. Josh disappears under the covers and starts to eat her out. Ada gets lost in the moment, when suddenly Josh stops and pokes his head out from under the covers.*

JOSH: And I'm sorry about the Frank stuff. You don't want to talk about him while you're in bed with me. I get it. So should we...?

ADA: YES, go back to doing THAT.

> *She pushes his head back under the covers.*

> *But now she's distracted and can't enjoy this. She pushes him away.*

It's just—I can't stop [thinking about Frank] —

> *Josh settles on his side of the bed, as Ada pulls the covers over herself.*

The last time I saw you guys at the hospital, the night we had coffee—
JOSH: Yeah?
ADA: —he was getting an angiogram, another fucking angiogram.
JOSH: I remember, I think.

> *Ada gets dressed, as she launches into...*

ADA: I haven't ever really talked to anyone about this.
So after you left,
Dr. O'Neil came by to tell me they thought he'd had a stroke.
They weren't sure,
but they thought it was a distinct possibility

and they had to do a CT scan
to find out how much damage it had done.

I remember Paul warned me they weren't big on hope.

So then he, like, tells me they're not gonna get to the CAT scan until the *next day*,
and then he leaves me there,
and you guys are gone, and I'm alone, and the hospital is a horrible place to be by yourself, you know?
JOSH: Right.
ADA: So I'm sitting there trying not to think about this fucking stroke news,
okay,
and I'm up all night
because I can't sleep, because I'm still at the hospital, and I'm just trying not to feel like the walls are falling, and then, the next morning, this family shows up.
They're loud and noisy and crying and talking and it's like:
thank God for this family, you know?
JOSH: Yeah.
ADA: This 20-year-old kid,
her name's Sarah,
she got hit by a fucking bus.
And her head's all caved in.
And like I said the whole family's there,

>like 20 people, aunts and uncles, everything, the whole deal.
>They're going through this tragedy and I'm happy.
>Because now I don't have to think about Frank's stroke.

JOSH: Wow.

ADA: Because these people are too loud,
>they fill up too much of the room.

JOSH: Right.

ADA: Suddenly I'm going out to the sandwich shop
>and buying food for everyone.
>Stuff like that.
>I'm useful, I'm helping them,
>kind of like
>the first day I was there,
>in that waiting room,
>how you guys took me under your wing,
>how you told me what to expect.
>Now I'm doing that for these people
>and it feels good.
>So much of the time you feel *so helpless*
>and for once it felt good to deal
>with someone else's problems.
>And not think about...you know.

JOSH: The inevitable.

ADA: So the day starts to move.
>And I'm not thinking about Frank,
>I'm not thinking about the stroke,

I'm doing my thing with these new people.
I'm showing them the ropes.
"This is what you need to ask the doctor,"
things like that.
And then suddenly it's seven o'clock
and Dr. O'Neil comes back.
And I'm not ready for this moment.
I am not fucking ready for this moment.
I've spent the whole day
not getting ready for this moment.
It's finally here
and I'm not ready.
But I can't stop the moment. He has to tell me.
I look at Sarah's mother.
She smiles at me
and I want to punch her in the face I hate her so much in
that moment.
I go out into the hall with Dr. O'Neil
and he tells me there was
definitely a stroke.
He tells me he's not going to sugarcoat it,
it's fucking bad.
I ask him: "how bad"
and he tells me "twenty percent."
I don't even know what that's supposed to mean.

I'm still holding my shit together at this point.

I just look at him and I'm like:

"what? WHAT? What does that mean, twenty percent?"

And he says: "I would say that Frank has a twenty percent chance of surviving today's stroke, at best."

JOSH: Fuck.

ADA: Right?

It's like a punch to my gut,

but I don't want to cry,

not in front of this doctor who thinks he knows everything,

I will not let him see me cry

because then twenty percent really means twenty percent.

If I give it that power,

then I'm saying I believe in his number,

but I'm not gonna believe in it,

no,

I'm gonna stay on the other side of his number.

The side of hope.

"You have to have hope."

The side of miracles.

That's the side I want to stay on.

JOSH: Yeah, of course. Right, of course.

ADA: So I don't cry. I don't give him a reaction.

But I can't stay at the hospital.

I walk out onto 12th Street

and that's when I realize

I've left my coat in the waiting room
and of course it's February
so it's freezing
but I can't go back up there,
so I just start walking.
I don't even really know where I'm going,
it's like my body's taking over
and I'm just moving.
I find myself standing right outside P.S. 122,
and I realize I'm missing my writing group.
Like, it's happening right now.
My body didn't know how to react to the day, I guess,
so it went into autopilot
and it came here.
And I haven't been to group in two weeks,
not since Frank had his aneurysm,
and I haven't even talked to any of these people,
none of them even know what's going on,
which almost feels like a blessing, right?
So I decide I'm gonna do this,
I need to do something normal, damnit.
So I go in,
and they've already started,
everyone's sitting around this table
and I quietly take my place.
Like my whole world isn't falling apart,

I just sit at the table.
And this guy David Starfis—
he's reading a chapter from this novel he's working on about
the Industrial Revolution and it's terrible,
but it's not really registering because
as I'm sitting there listening
...it's the first time
all day
that I've let my brain stop,
you know?
I've been going and going and going and going
and trying not to be afraid
and trying not to think about
all the terrible things that might happen
and then one of those terrible things happens
and I've been holding my breathe all day
and this is
the first time
that I've let it go.
And I start to feel it in my throat.
This heaviness,
the whole day building up. Inside my throat.
And that's when I realize...

JOSH: You're gonna throw up.
ADA: I'm gonna throw up!
JOSH: I knew you were gonna say that!

ADA: I am going to throw the fuck up.

    And I am going to do it RIGHT NOW.

    I try to get out,

    but there isn't enough time.

    Because as soon as I stand up,

    it starts.

    I throw up.

    David Starfis doesn't even know what hit him.

    I take a few more steps toward the door

    and I throw up again.

JOSH: Holy fuck, this is crazy.

ADA: And then again.

    And then I reach the door

    and I throw up there too,

    and then again out in the hall,

    and then again at the front door,

    and again out on the sidewalk,

    and then again down the street.

    I throw up, like, eight times.

    It's the most disgusting thing ever.

    Vomit everywhere.

    But after the eighth time,

    I actually start to feel better.

JOSH: Like you cleaned your system.

ADA: Right, like, I suddenly feel like whatever God's gonna throw my way, whatever happens to Frank, I'm gonna be able to deal with it. It's like a whole new world again, and I start to feel hopeful.

I know it's weird, but it's what I feel.

Because if he can survive this,

when they're only giving him a twenty percent chance,

then he could survive anything.

We just have to get through *this*.

He could live. It might happen.

That's what I started to feel...

JOSH: What happened to Sarah?

ADA: Who?

JOSH: The girl who got hit by the bus.

ADA: Oh. Right. Totally brain-dead. Anyway...

JOSH: Well Frank looked really good at dinner. I know he's having a hard time, but—

ADA: You're doing it again, you're talking about him.

JOSH: Sorry...

ADA: When I said we're not gonna talk about him, I meant you, you're not gonna talk about him.

JOSH: I get it.

ADA: I should get going soon. So could you just fuck my brains out a little bit, one more time, right now? Okay?

JOSH: Okay.

Lights shift.

TRACK 10:

"I'm So Tired"

Julia's bedroom. Julia and Paul lie on the bed, listening to the White Album.

PAUL: God, today sucked. If I never have to see another hospital...

JULIA: At least the waiting room outside the ER has better chairs.

PAUL: And the vending machine works.

JULIA: Did you ever think a working vending machine would be one of your criteria for a good day?

PAUL: No.

JULIA: Thank God it was just a seizure.

PAUL: She didn't take her meds last night. That's why it happened.

JULIA: You're sure?

PAUL: Pretty sure.

They listen to the Beatles for a beat.

JULIA: Remember how she and dad used to listen to this at night after they'd put us to bed? I used to sing along, quietly, as I was falling asleep. I'd try to stay awake until "my" song came on, but I was usually out cold by "Bungalow Bill."

PAUL: You know the *White Album* was their sex album, right?

JULIA: What? No. Don't say that.

PAUL: It's true!

JULIA: I don't want to know that.

PAUL: If they had the *White Album* on—

JULIA: My pure childhood memories...

PAUL: —it meant they were doing it.

JULIA: ...are completely tainted.

PAUL: Our mom is a sex fiend.

JULIA: It's so disgusting.

PAUL: Sgt. Pepper meant they were fighting.

JULIA: Well I knew that. Obviously. She doesn't even listen to the Beatles anymore. Not like she used to. Have you noticed that?

PAUL: Do you ever...miss what she was like before the aneurysm?

JULIA: She's not nice like she used to be.

PAUL: I know, right?

JULIA: That's the thing that trips me out the most.

PAUL: What if you hadn't been with her? When she had the aneurysm?

JULIA: I can't even...

PAUL: She'd be dead. No question about it.

JULIA: We were doing the dishes. Can you imagine how upset she would have been if she died before finishing the dishes? Not that she'd care anymore...

PAUL: Remember that thing she and I used to do, where I'd be like, "I'm hungry, I feel like Mexican food," or whatever. And she'd grab my arm and say—

JULIA (*grabbing his arm*): "You don't feel like Mexican food to me." So stupid.

PAUL: It wasn't stupid.

JULIA: It was a little stupid.

PAUL: Okay, fine, a little. But it was our thing. I tried to do it with her the other day, and she wouldn't do it. I don't know if she didn't remember, or if she just wouldn't play along.

JULIA: "You don't feel like a chicken fajita."

PAUL: Okay, enough.

JULIA: How'd that even start? It's so dumb!

PAUL: I know, you're right, it is!

JULIA: "You don't feel like a cheese enchilada."

She starts tickling him.

PAUL: Stop it!

JULIA: I can't believe you're still ticklish!

She pins him. He tries to break free, but her tickling is too strong. Josh enters. Paul and Julia stop the tickle fight when they see him.

JOSH: Your mom's asleep.

JULIA: Did she take her meds?

JOSH: Yeah.

JULIA: Because Paul doesn't think she took them last night.

PAUL: She didn't.

JULIA: Which is why she had the seizure.

JOSH: She took them. I'm gonna watch *The Daily Show*. Go back to your brother-sister weirdness.

JULIA: There is nothing weird about a tickle fight.

Josh exits.

PAUL: Do I sense tension?

JULIA: "You don't feel like a fish burrito."

PAUL: I'm being serious.

JULIA: I know you are. I was ignoring you.

PAUL: Wanna talk about it?

JULIA: I want to talk to mom about it.

PAUL: Then talk to her.

JULIA: *Old* mom.

PAUL: Oh.

JULIA: She's the one I want to talk to.

He holds her hand. They lay back and listen to the Beatles for a few beats.

Lights shift.

TRACK 11:
"Take These Broken Wings"

A few days later.

Ada and Frank's apartment.

Frank on the phone, a takeout menu in his hands.

Ada listens from the doorway, unseen by Frank.

FRANK (*struggling with the words*): Hi, hello...could I...sorry, wait, could I...

(*effortlessly*)

This is so hard to say, damn it.

(*struggling again*)

Could I...sorry...yes, order, yes:

(*practicing the word*)

Order, order, order. Could I?

> *Beat, waiting for a response.*

Hello?

> *But there's no one there, he hangs up the phone.*

Damn it.

> *He dials again.*

Hi, hello...could I...order?

> *Beat.*

Thank you, I want a small pizza with pepperoni.

> *Shit, that was wrong.*

No, damn it. Sorry, no, that's wrong, never mind.

> *He hangs up.*

Damn it. Damn it, damn it, damn it.

Ada comes in and sits with Frank.

ADA: Did you call the pizza place?

FRANK: Yeah.

ADA: How'd you do?

FRANK: Not good.

ADA: Did you place the order?

FRANK: No, she didn't want that.

ADA: Who's "she"? Who are you talking about?

FRANK: Me.

ADA: You're not a "she," you're a "he."

FRANK: I know that.

ADA: Okay, but you gotta say the right word.

FRANK: I know.

ADA: And you're talking in the first person, so you should actually say "I didn't want that."

FRANK: Fuck, sorry:
   I, I, I.

ADA: Good, that's right. "I didn't want that." Say it.

FRANK: I didn't want that.

ADA: Good, okay. So...you ordered the wrong thing, what did you order that you didn't want?

He points at something on the menu.

A small pizza?

FRANK: Yeah, but I didn't actually do it.

ADA: I'm hungry too, so we should get a medium.

FRANK: I know, that's what I'm saying! I didn't do it. *Medium. Medium.* But I didn't even do it, it wasn't what she wanted.

ADA: Stop with the "she." We just went over that, you're still talking about yourself—

FRANK: Yes.

ADA: It wasn't what you wanted.

FRANK: "It wasn't what you wanted."

ADA: Okay, no, you have to say "I" when you're talking in the first person.

FRANK: I know, it's all in my head that way, but it just doesn't—

ADA: —I'm not being a bitch—

FRANK: —come out right.

(*re: she's not being a bitch*)

I know.

ADA: We'll keep working on that one. When you're talking about yourself, you use "I." And you're a "he." Those are the two things you have to get.

FRANK: I know. *I know it.* It's just difficult.

ADA: I know. But we'll get there.

Ada pauses for a beat. Talking with Frank can be exhausting.

She takes a breath.

So what did you order? Show me on the menu.

He points at another part of the menu.

You ordered pepperoni?
FRANK: Yeah. I mean, *no*. But that's what I told the guy on the phone.
ADA: That was such a good sentence. See, when you stop thinking so hard about what you're trying to say, the words come out.
FRANK: I know.
ADA: But you're a vegetarian.
FRANK: I know!
ADA: So I don't think you want pepperoni.
FRANK: That's exactly what I'm saying.
ADA: You like mushrooms, that's what you want.
FRANK: Yes, that. Exactly!

He hands her the phone.

You order it.
ADA: Okay, no, I just said the word, you can do it too. You're doing this, you're ordering dinner. Now what's the word I just said? Say what you want. Say it.

Frank gives her an annoyed look.

What?

FRANK: I'm done with therapy today.

ADA: This isn't therapy, we're having a conversation. I can't help it if I correct you here and there. I can't turn that part of me off. Don't fucking give up. Say the word. Say it.

FRANK: Goddamnit.

ADA: Frank, please.

FRANK: ...pepperoni.

ADA: No...

FRANK: I'm tired.

ADA: Come on, you can do it, I'm amazed by all the things that come out of your mouth lately. You can say this one stupid little word.

FRANK: I can't.

ADA: Come on.

(*sounding it out*)

Muuuuuh...muuhhhhshhhh—

FRANK: —room. Mushroom.

ADA: Right. Good. Mushroom.

FRANK: Mushroom.

ADA: See!

FRANK: I know.

ADA: Now call them back.

FRANK: No, you.

ADA: No, you got into this mess with the pizza people, you call them back.

FRANK: I already told you, I'm done with therapy today.

ADA: Damn it, Frank, this isn't therapy, it's dinner.

FRANK: You call them, I don't want to do it.

ADA: I'm not calling them, so if you wanna eat—

FRANK: Okay, fine.

ADA: Thank you.

He picks up the phone, dials.

FRANK: Hi, hello...could I...yes, order, thank you...

Beat.

Yes...a small pizza with pepperoni.

He knows he got it wrong, but he can't take it back. Fuck.

Okay, thanks...pickup...thanks, okay.

He hangs up.

Sorry, that was wrong. I said the wrong—

ADA: No, it's okay. You did good. You tried. I'll eat the pepperoni off the top. And if you want something else, I can make a salad. You're doing really good.

She starts to cry. This is all so hard. He reaches for her, but she turns away.

I'm okay. I'm sorry. Just give me a second.
FRANK: Here. I have something.

He reaches into his pocket. Pulls out a little orange. Offers it to Ada.

ADA: A sad orange?
FRANK: Don't be...sad. Give it to...sad orange.

She laughs. Takes the orange, grateful. Frank puts his hand on her thigh.

ADA: Julia called. She wants to have us over for dinner again. I don't really want to go.
FRANK: No, we should go. We should. They're good people. It's good for us to go out. We need that. We should definitely go.

Ada wants to say something about how good those sentences were.

ADA: Okay. We'll go.

Frank moves his hand up Ada's leg, inside her skirt.

What are you doing?
FRANK: Can I?
ADA: Of course, yes, I'm sorry, you don't need...

She hasn't been touched like this by Frank in a long time and it feels good.

She lets out a little moan.

...to ask for permission.
FRANK: Now can I...
ADA: No, seriously, you don't need to ask for permission.

He stops touching her.

FRANK: No, I need to ask you something else.
ADA: Oh, okay.
FRANK: I've been practicing this...
      ...what I want to say.
ADA: What is it?
FRANK: It's just, I was wondering...Before the aneurysm...

ADA (*patient, coaxing*): What are you trying to say?

FRANK: Can she...That's wrong, I mean...

ADA: You can get it...

FRANK: *Can I...*

ADA: Good, that's good.

FRANK: ...marry you? You already said yes, before the aneurysm, but I didn't know, if you still...will you still?

(*getting the words out again, better this time*)

Can I marry you.

ADA: Yes. Frank, yes, of course. Of course you can marry me.

She kisses him.

FRANK: It's hard.

ADA: I know it is, but it'll get easier...

FRANK: No, I mean...

ADA: What? Oh...

You're hard.

FRANK: I'm hard.

ADA: And there is a God. Thank you.

She kisses him again.

Lights shift.

TRACK 12:

"A Damn Good Whacking"

A few days later. A subway car. Josh and Mary Jean sit together.

MARY JEAN: I hate you. I do. I really do.

JOSH: You've said.

MARY JEAN: I'm saying it again.

JOSH: You've said it about ten times.

MARY JEAN: In case it hasn't gotten through your thick skull.

JOSH: I got it. You hate me. It's cool.

MARY JEAN: So will you leave me alone?

JOSH: I promised Julia I'd get you there...

MARY JEAN: So...?

JOSH: So no. I'm gonna get you to the doctor's office, I'm gonna make sure everything goes fine, and then I'm gonna get you home.

MARY JEAN: He's not a doctor, he's a physical therapist.

JOSH: Still...

MARY JEAN: You see, that's why I hate you. You're stubborn.

JOSH: I'm just doing what Julia told me to do.

MARY JEAN: And you're robotic, robot-like, you can't think for yourself, like a robot.

JOSH: You can't offend me. I'm gonna see that you get to your doctor no matter what.

MARY JEAN: My physical therapist.

JOSH: Whichever.

MARY JEAN: I know how to use the subway.

JOSH: I didn't say you didn't.

MARY JEAN: God, I really do hate you. I could hit you right now, that's how much I hate you. I just want to whack you in the head.

JOSH: Hate me, hit me, whatever.

MARY JEAN: I just, I try to figure out what she sees in you. You must be good in bed, that's all I can figure.

JOSH: Wow.

MARY JEAN: Are you good in bed?

JOSH: I don't really want to have this conversation.

MARY JEAN: And I don't want to be escorted to my doctor's office—

JOSH: Your physical therapist's office—

MARY JEAN: Fine, whatever, yes, my physical therapist's office, fuck you, anyway, here we are, so: are you good in bed?

JOSH: You're really asking me that?

MARY JEAN: I wanna know what my daughter sees in you. Why she ever bothered to marry you. So...

JOSH: ...yeah.

MARY JEAN: Yeah?

JOSH: Yeah.

MARY JEAN: You are? Because you don't look it—

JOSH: Thanks—

MARY JEAN: —but that's all I could figure.

JOSH: I mean, yeah—I'm good. This is making me uncomfortable, this conversation.

MARY JEAN: Good. But you make her happy? That's the point.

JOSH: Well, more than just in bed.

MARY JEAN: I didn't mean "just in bed." You make her happy—

JOSH: —in general, yeah. Sometimes.

MARY JEAN: Sometimes? Why "sometimes"?

JOSH: Well it's obviously been difficult lately. Things are strained. If you haven't noticed.

MARY JEAN: Then you need to work harder. If I die tomorrow, I need to know my daughter's happy.

JOSH: Don't say things like that.

MARY JEAN: What, it's true. My head could explode.

JOSH: Seriously, don't say that.

MARY JEAN: It happened once, it could happen again.

JOSH: But I don't want to think about things like that.

MARY JEAN: You're saying you like me? That's why you don't want to think about it?

JOSH: Honestly?

MARY JEAN: Honestly.

JOSH: No. But Julia does, so...

MARY JEAN: So you want what she wants?

JOSH: I don't want her to lose you.

MARY JEAN: That's a good answer. Better answer than "sometimes." You know, the other day was the first seizure I've had in three months. So you know what that means, don't you...?

JOSH: No.

MARY JEAN: It means I got one out of the way. The possibility I'm gonna have another one so soon? It's not very likely. So...you think you could make me happy like you make Julia happy?

JOSH: I'm not having sex with you.

MARY JEAN: Oh God no—

JOSH: If that's what you—

MARY JEAN: That's not what I meant—

JOSH: Good.

MARY JEAN: I meant: could you have some compassion for me? You're an actor. Put yourself in my place.

JOSH: Like an acting exercise?

MARY JEAN: Sure.

JOSH: Okay, I can do that. So...I'm a sixty-*ish*-year-old woman.

MARY JEAN: Fifty-five.

JOSH: Really?

MARY JEAN: Well, as long as we're pretending.

JOSH: So I'm a fifty-five-year-old woman. I have two kids. And a son-in-law who I find difficult. And I had this aneurysm that basically changed the playing field. I'm living with my whole family again. And I get seizures sometimes. It's incredibly difficult. My whole world's different.

MARY JEAN: And I want to go to the physical therapist's office alone.

JOSH: Right. I want to know I can get there, that I can ride the subway like I've done my entire life.

MARY JEAN: My entire life.

JOSH: That if I have another seizure, today, alone—if I die on the way to the therapist's office—I'm okay with that.

MARY JEAN: I am. I'm okay.

JOSH: I just want a little independence.

MARY JEAN: I don't want to beg.

JOSH: No, I don't want to beg. Especially not to this actor guy who my daughter married foolishly, impulsively, probably stupidly. Begging him is the last thing I want.

MARY JEAN: I want to feel like a normal person.

JOSH: Right. And damn my brain for not letting me feel that way. Damn the seizure from the other day for making people baby me again. Damn my leg for only being at eighty percent and making me need therapy in the first place. Damn it, but I don't want a babysitter. I don't need a babysitter.

MARY JEAN: I don't.

JOSH: The train's stopping. The door's opening. And I wish my son-in-law would walk out that door. Would get off the train. Would leave me, so I could do this on my own. Okay.

MARY JEAN: Thank you.

He goes.

Lights shift.

TRACK 13:

"She and Her Man"

Frank and Ada's apartment. Julia enters, with tupperware.

JULIA: Frank? Ada? Are either of you home? Hello?

FRANK (*from off-stage*): Hold on!

JULIA: Sorry! No one answered when I knocked, and the door was unlocked, so I walked right in!

Frank enters, wearing nothing but a towel. He's wet, fresh from the shower.

FRANK: Sorry.

JULIA: You were in the shower—

FRANK: Yeah.

JULIA: I'm sorry, I can come back, this is a bad time.

FRANK: No, stay, just—

JULIA: I'll wait in here, you get dressed. I'm sorry I barged in, the door was unlocked.

FRANK: Oh. It was?

JULIA: Yeah, you really shouldn't leave it unlocked.

FRANK: It was [Ada] —it wasn't [me] —it was [Ada] —I was in the shower—when he...when he...when *she* left.

JULIA: Of course, Ada started her new job, didn't she? With Scholastic? She must have left when you were in the shower?

FRANK: Right.

JULIA: I didn't realize today was [her first day] —I thought I'd catch both of you. Why don't you go get dressed? I'll be fine. Take your time.

FRANK: Okay, thanks.

He exits.

JULIA: I brought you some food! It's nothing special! Just leftover stuffing and yams. And a pumpkin pie we never even touched. I know you skipped Thanksgiving. I wish you'd accepted my invitation. We would have enjoyed your company. There's a lot to be thankful for this last year...I know it doesn't always seem that way—I know it's tough, the day to day stuff, but...I left Josh. It was an ordeal. But it feels right, I think. No, I know: it's all for the best.

Frank re-enters, now dressed.

So, as I was saying, I brought you leftovers. There's enough here for you and Ada to have at least two meals each.

FRANK: Thank you. Let me [take it] —

JULIA: I can put everything in the fridge, if you want—

FRANK: No, please—

JULIA: It's really no trouble—
FRANK: *Please*. Let me.

> *He takes the bag with his good hand.*
> *Exits.*

JULIA: I'm jealous of Ada and her new job! Editor sounds so glamorous. I know Ada would say it isn't, but it still sounds nice. I'm thinking of giving up acting. I shouldn't complain, I shot another episode of *Law and Order*. I got raped and shoved into a trunk, and then I got to play dead in the morgue scene. I think I might start teaching pilates.

> *Frank comes back in with two beers and a bottle opener.*

FRANK: Here, help me, I can't.
JULIA: Beer? It's eight-thirty in the morning.
FRANK: You need it.
JULIA: The Josh thing?

> *Frank nods. Julia pops open her beer. Frank holds his out and she pops that one open too. They take long swigs.*

He's been pulling away for a while. I don't think he could ever handle the thing with my mom.

FRANK: Can you?

JULIA: I can handle it.

>*She takes another swig. He does too.*

FRANK: This is good.

>*He gives her a smile.*

You know? It's good, this. I'm so glad you...I mean, that we...God, how do I say this?

JULIA: Take your time...

FRANK: I'm so glad that you and I, that you and I...you know. When we...what's the [word]?...Here, let me—

>*He takes her hand, flattens out her palm. Draws the outline of a letter.*

JULIA: S...?

>*He nods. Outlines a few more letters.*

T...A...R...B...Starbucks?

FRANK: Yes! Thank you!

JULIA: You're glad we bumped into each other at Starbucks?

FRANK: Yes! The thing that's weird, to me, is—we live—

(*motioning*)

—there—and here.

JULIA: We live so close to each other.

FRANK: Yeah. And it's weird that it took so long for us to meet each other. Since we're neighbors. Not that I would have known who you were because I was, after my aneurysm...coma. But I'm glad we met because you're a really good...a really good friend. It's weird. My people, my...how do you [say it]?

JULIA: Your family?

FRANK: Yeah, they live far away. We don't talk. So...I don't really have much—not too many people—but...I have a lot.

> *He sighs, slightly embarrassed. Talking can be exhausting sometimes.*

JULIA: You're talking so much better than you were just two months ago when we met. Really, you are.

> *He shakes his head, not really believing it. Takes a swig of beer.*

Do you think, maybe...I know you already have a speech therapist, but...he gives you homework, right? I could help.

He gives her a look, slightly dubious.

It wouldn't be a charity thing, more like a friend thing. You were right about beer-in-the-morning. This is nice. I'm gonna have to do this more often, we both can. Next time on a Saturday morning with Ada. But now I should go, so—I'll call you about the speech therapy thing, okay?
FRANK: Okay.

She exits.

Lights shift.

TRACK 14:
"Why I'm By Myself"

A restaurant. Ada's sitting, looking at the menu, alone, when: Josh approaches.

JOSH: Can we talk?

ADA: Josh? What are you doing here?

JOSH: I was walking by. Something caught my eye. I turned and looked through the window. And there you were.

ADA: Why did you come in here?

JOSH: It can't be an accident.

ADA: *What* can't be an accident?

JOSH: That I happened to turn and look through the window at the exact moment when you'd be sitting here and I'd see you. Things like that don't happen unless they're supposed to—

ADA: Josh—

JOSH: It's what they call fate, one of those fated moments.

ADA: No, it's not.

JOSH: Paul said this thing once about how coincidences are the universe's way of being lazy or something. But how can the universe be lazy? Me bumping into you? This is not a coincidence. There's no such thing. When we met in the waiting room: that was fate. That was destiny. We were—

ADA: I can't do this right now. Frank's in the bathroom. He'll be back any minute.

JOSH: I miss you.

ADA: It's been months, Josh.

JOSH: So?

ADA: So it's dead, let it die.

JOSH: I left Julia.

ADA: I don't believe you.

JOSH: Okay, she left me. But I was gonna leave her first, remember—the day her mom's head exploded—and that's gotta count for something. We were wrong together. But you and I, you and I were right together.

ADA: No, we weren't—

JOSH: We had a thing. The hotel thing.

ADA: We didn't. We had sex three times.

JOSH: That's a "thing!"

ADA: It's not a "thing," it's an affair. And it's over.

JOSH: Okay, first: it was five times. And second: you loved being with me, I know you did. Why are you acting like you didn't?

ADA: Okay, *first,* Frank is in the bathroom, thirty feet away, so I can't do this right now. And second...

JOSH: Yes? And? Second?

ADA: I was falling apart. You were there, you were what I needed, and I'll always be grateful for that. But you're crazy if you think what we had was right. It was all kinds of wrong—

JOSH: No—

ADA: —and that's all it was. Really, truly.

JOSH: Right. And I put you back together, like a prince.

ADA: Do you even hear how insane you sound?

JOSH: I shed a little bit of light on those dark times for you—

ADA: But that "light" is out now, I've got another "light," so: you have to go. You have to stop this. I don't want you in my life. I'm sorry to be harsh.

JOSH: I like when you're harsh.

ADA: You obviously require it.

JOSH: That's one of the things I like about you.

ADA: Please, Josh. Before Frank comes back.

JOSH: I'm moving to California.

ADA: Okay...

JOSH: Come with me.

ADA: Stop, stop this—

JOSH: You're not supposed to be with Frank.

ADA: This is ridiculous.

JOSH: You'll end up being his caretaker forever and you'll regret it. I'm just saying.

ADA: We're married.

JOSH: What?

ADA: We got married. Two weeks ago. I love him.

JOSH: Oh.

Frank enters. Sees Josh.

FRANK: Hey.

JOSH: Hi Frank. Good to see you, you look good.

(*no response*)

Great. Okay, well. Good to see both of you.

FRANK: Josh.

JOSH: Yeah?

FRANK: If you, if you, you know?

JOSH: No, I'm sorry, I don't know what you're trying to say.

FRANK: If you...fuck.

JOSH: It's okay, just take your time.

FRANK: No. If you...fuck...my wife...again? If you do it, again? You're dead.

JOSH: Okay. Right. Good to know. I should probably, you know—go.

FRANK: Yeah.

JOSH: Anyway, yeah, it was good to see both of—you. So—

FRANK: Bye.

JOSH: Enjoy your meal.

He hurries out.

FRANK: Now what...should we...order?

Lights shift.

TRACK 15:

"Why Don't We?"

Starbucks. Ada and Julia sit together.

ADA: Thank you for meeting me here.

JULIA: Any time. You sounded—

ADA: I was weird on the phone, I know, I'm sorry—

JULIA: Yeah, you sounded upset.

ADA: I don't have girlfriends. I've always been a one-of-the-guys kind of girl. But I've been so grateful for...

JULIA: I'm glad we're friends too.

ADA: ...you've been there for Frank. And it's so nice of you and—

JULIA: Don't worry about it. I like him. I'm happy to do what I can.

ADA: About that...It's great you're helping him out. I don't want you to think I'm not doing enough. That I'm selfish with my time. But I love Frank so much, and—and I can't do it all. Because I don't want to resent him, I just want to love him.

JULIA: That's not selfish. I get that.

ADA: That's why I called. To make sure you [understood]. And I wanted to have another girl date.

JULIA: If you're expecting me to put out, you're too late. I left my experimental phase in college.

ADA: You had an experimental phase?

JULIA: Veronica Goldberg. She wrote poetry. She was my Resident Advisor, freshman year. An older woman. I broke her heart.

We're friends on Facebook now. Which is so depressing.

ADA: How are you, Julia?

JULIA: You're asking about the Josh stuff?

ADA: Yeah. Are you coping? Are you angry? Are you sad?

JULIA: Am I coping? I think so. Am I angry? Yes. Am I sad? Of course I am. Did I love him? Deeply. Were we right for each other? I really don't think we were. Does that make any of this easy? Not at all. That's...that's how I am.

ADA: You'll find someone else—

JULIA: You don't need to do that. I'm okay alone. For now. I'm not looking to jump into anything.

ADA: Of course.

Beat.

So, this is the Starbucks where you and Frank bumped into each other, isn't it?

JULIA: No, it was the one five blocks up.

ADA: Really? When I hear the story, this is the Starbucks I see in my head. Oh God, no, I'm sorry, fuck, I can't do this.

JULIA: Do what?

ADA: Lie to you. I have to come clean. I like you too much.

JULIA: Wait, stop. Whatever you think you have to say—

ADA: It's not good, Julia. What I'm gonna say. It's not good—

JULIA: You don't have to say it. Really.

ADA: But I do. I'm sorry. I have to.

JULIA: You don't.

ADA: It's about Josh.

JULIA: I don't want to hear it.

ADA: But I want to be a good friend—

JULIA: Really—let's not have some weird confession-at-Starbucks.

ADA: —because *you're* such a good friend and—

JULIA: And I want to stay that way. Look I—I have suspicions. I have thoughts in my head. Guesses about what you might say—

ADA: I need to get it off my chest.

JULIA: And if you say what I'm afraid you're gonna say, you won't be able to take it back and we'll fight and we'll end up hating each other. I don't want to hate you. I don't have girlfriends either and I need a friend. So let's stop talking. Why don't we do that? Pretend the words are lost in the deep recesses of your brain and don't try to find them.

ADA: But—

JULIA: I'm serious. Don't say the words. I don't want to change what we have and those words will change this.

> *Ada hears what she's saying. They both stop talking. Take a sip of their coffees in silence.*
>
> *Lights shift.*

TRACK 16:
"I Will"

St. Luke's Hospital. The waiting room. Mary Jean and Paul enter.

MARY JEAN: This is it?

PAUL: I can't believe Kathy isn't here.

MARY JEAN: Who's Kathy again?

PAUL: The nurse you liked.

MARY JEAN: The cunt?

PAUL: Mom, *please*.

MARY JEAN: What?

PAUL: I told you not to say words like that.

MARY JEAN: Well excuse me for living. Why do you care if she's here?

PAUL: Because I want her to see you. To see how well you're doing.

MARY JEAN: You should have called ahead. Found out when she was working.

PAUL: She must have switched shifts.

MARY JEAN: I could care less, is all—

PAUL: Mom—

MARY JEAN: I'm just saying: if you really wanted to see her, you should have called ahead. Because you're the one who liked her, not me. Me, I don't even really remember her.

PAUL: But you do.

MARY JEAN: I don't—

PAUL: At first we thought she was a total bitch. She never smiled. You want the nurses to smile occasionally because when they smile you start to think things are gonna turn out okay. When they're serious, your head spins into worst case scenarios—

MARY JEAN: I would think that your mother in a coma about to die is already the worst case scenario.

PAUL: —but then I started to notice how attentive she was. Like: some nurses, they'd let your heart rate machine beep for ten minutes before doing anything about it, but Nurse Kathy? She was always on it, right away.

MARY JEAN: I don't remember.

PAUL: You start to appreciate those little things when you're in here all day.

MARY JEAN: I was in a coma.

PAUL: But you have to remember, after you woke up, some of it.

MARY JEAN: She's a cunt, that's what I remember.

PAUL: Okay, I'm not even going to [argue anymore] —moving on. This is the waiting room.

MARY JEAN: I gathered.

PAUL: Is that how this is gonna be? You're gonna give me attitude the whole time we're here?

MARY JEAN: Maybe.

PAUL: Because I'm doing this for you, but we can leave. We can go right now. Or you can be nice to me. Try to be nice. Because I'm being nice, bringing you here. Your personal timeline is missing twenty-four days and I'm trying to fill in the missing pieces, and that's a nice thing. Try to be nice back. Just try. But we can go. If that's what you want.

MARY JEAN (*trying to put in some effort*): ...where would you sit?

PAUL: Here. This was my chair, my spot.

MARY JEAN: And Julia? Where would she...

PAUL: Sometimes she'd sit next to me. Sometimes she'd sit over there, so she could see the TV.

MARY JEAN: So you and Julia, the two of you were in here for twenty-four days, waiting for me to wake up.

PAUL: Well, you woke up on day twelve—

MARY JEAN: But still—

PAUL: But you didn't move to the 4th floor until day twenty-four, so yeah. This is where we were the first twenty-four days.

MARY JEAN: Twenty-four days in this room? That's horrifying.

Beat.

How long are you going to be here?

PAUL: Be more specific.

MARY JEAN: How long are you going to be in New York?

PAUL: As long as you need me.

MARY JEAN: Then I want you to go. I need you to go.

PAUL: Where?

MARY JEAN: Back to Boston. I don't need you.

PAUL: But you could have a re-bleed. You could have a seizure while climbing some stairs and then fall. You could—
MARY JEAN: I have Julia for all of those things.
PAUL: But—
MARY JEAN: This isn't up for discussion.
PAUL: I wanna be here for you. If I go back to Boston, I'll feel useless, like a total tool, just—

She grabs his arm.

MARY JEAN: "You don't feel like a total tool to me." That used to work better when we were talking about food. I'm rusty.
PAUL: No, it worked.
MARY JEAN: You're gonna blink and then realize you've taken care of me your whole life. I don't want that to happen to you. You put everything on hold to come out here. Go back to Boston and be a teacher again. Do good things. Would you do that for me?
PAUL: I will.
MARY JEAN: Then let's go. This place creeps the living fuck out of me.

Lights shift.

TRACK 17:
"Julia"

Frank and Ada's apartment. Frank sits with Julia, who has flash cards.

FRANK: [reads first flash card]

JULIA: Good. Next.

FRANK: [he repeats the first flash card]

JULIA: No, that was the last one, look at this one.

FRANK: [reads new flash card correctly]

JULIA: Good.

FRANK: Uh...it's...oh I know it, it's...fuck.

JULIA: You can do it.

FRANK: I know but it's just difficult. I mean, it's stupid because I know it, but I can't [say it]...

JULIA: I know, but you can get it. The word's in there. Try again.

FRANK: [repeats the first flash card]?

JULIA: Now you're guessing. Sound out the word. [She helps him sound out the word]

FRANK: [he correctly reads the flash card, with Julia's help]

JULIA: See, I told you it was in there.

FRANK: Can we do something else?

JULIA: You don't like the flashcards?

FRANK: No. Tell me about you. How are you?

JULIA: You're the one who's supposed to practice talking, not me.

FRANK: But your...what's the word? How is he?

JULIA: My mom?

FRANK: Yeah, how is he?

JULIA: She's good. I guess. I don't know. She's fine. How's Ada?

FRANK (*re: Julia's mom*): He's not good?

JULIA: What do you mean? Is something wrong with Ada, is she—

FRANK: No, not Ada. I mean, your—what's the word? Your, your—

JULIA: We're still talking about my mom?

FRANK: Yeah. He's not good?

JULIA: She's fine. That's what I said. She basically has her full range of motion again, and she's getting around, she's out in the world, she's doing her own thing, she's great.

FRANK: But you don't sound...real. How is he really?

JULIA: She's...I love her because she's my mom.

FRANK: But...

JULIA: Josh is gone. Paul went back home to Boston. So now it's just me and her in that apartment and I don't know what I'm doing with my life. It feels right, mostly. We're figuring out our new thing, how to make it work. She's different. Not the mom I'm used to. It's almost like she's my roommate now. My roommate who I love a lot. That's a horrible thing to say.

FRANK: No, it's not, it's—

JULIA: It is.

FRANK: It's...real.

JULIA: I guess. It feels bad. I don't want to seem ungrateful—she's alive and that's amazing, but—

FRANK: It's difficult.

JULIA: Yeah.

FRANK: Is your name, is it—

JULIA: It's Julia.

FRANK: I know. [Duh] *Hello*. What I mean is—

JULIA: —sorry, of course / you know—

FRANK: Are you...are you named after...you know?

JULIA: No, I'm sorry, I don't—

FRANK: "Half of what I say is meaningless...

But I say it just to reach you Juuuuulia."

JULIA: The Beatles song.

FRANK: Is that you?

JULIA: Am I named after that song?

FRANK: Yeah, that's what I...

JULIA: Yeah...actually.

FRANK: Wow.

JULIA: No one knows that song anymore. Mom was a Beatles freak. Is a Beatles freak. John Lennon's mom was named Julia, she died when John was a teenager, hit by a car. It's one of those things you never get over. My mom sang it to me when I was little, a lullaby. I remember thinking someone wrote it with me in mind, before I was born. They knew I'd be coming into the world. It made me feel like I was supposed to be here.

FRANK: So she gave you that.

Julia takes that in.

Should we...

JULIA: Back to the flashcards?

FRANK: Okay. [reads the flash card correctly]

JULIA: That's right. Good.

Lights shift.

END OF SIDE TWO

B-SIDE: EPILOGUE

Julia's kitchen. Julia's preparing dinner for her and her mom. She pauses and looks out at the audience.

JULIA: Hey.

It's me, again.

Julia.

I haven't really done this in awhile. Talked to you. Not since the hospital.

But I guess it would be selfish of me to only do this prayer thing when I need something.

I was on the phone with Paul the other night and he said he pictures you with John Lennon's face, but I can't do that. I was always a George Harrison girl. I know. I'm weird. Besides, I don't like to think of you with just one face. You're in everyone I meet. It's easier to see you that way. In all the faces.

I keep having this memory:

I'm 9-years-old. Paul and I spend the summer planting a garden in the alley by our house. It's Paul's idea. He sees possibility everywhere. We don't have a yard but there's this patch of dirt next to the house, so that's where we work.

Mom warns us not to get our hopes up. There's not much sun in the alley, she says. She tells us nothing's going to grow. But I don't care: my hopes are up anyway.

We work so hard on that garden. After several weeks, we have to admit mom's right—there's no sun, nothing will grow.

Then one morning we wake up and find these buckets filled with dirt on the cement patio out back, where all the sun is. Mom tells us: "This can be your garden." It's not at all what we expected, and it still takes us what feels like forever, but by the end of the summer, we have the most incredible, odd—but beautiful—collection of plants.

Yesterday—Valentine's Day—was Frank and Ada's wedding. Their second wedding, actually. The one they invited friends to. They wrote their own vows. It was beautiful. Paul flew out with his new boyfriend, the first one I've ever met. I brought my mom as my date. We're both ready to start seeing other people.

At the reception, the center piece on each of the tables was a bucket of these little oranges. The ones you can wrap your fingers around. I know the oranges were supposed to have some sort of significance, and I remember Ada saying something about oranges to me once, but honestly: I don't remember what it was. I mean, I can't keep everything in my head and I didn't even have brain trauma, you know? Regardless, they never explained why these buckets of oranges were meaningful. Maybe it was something they wanted to keep for themselves and share at the same time. Next to each bucket, there was a note that said: "*Please eat one.*"

So I did.

And it made me happy. That stupid little orange. I can't explain why that is. Maybe it was just the company: being with all these people I love.

And after everything we've been through.
After everything we continue to go through.
I just want to tell you that:

My hopes are up. For all of us.

Lights fade.

END OF PLAY

About the Playwright

ERIK PATTERSON is an award-winning playwright, screenwriter, and writing teacher.

His play, *One of the Nice Ones*, earned the Los Angeles Drama Critics Circle Award. His theater work has been produced or developed by Playwrights' Arena, the Los Angeles Theatre Centre, Theatre of NOTE, the Evidence Room, The Actors' Gang, the Echo Theater Company, the Lark Play Development Center, Moving Arts, Black Dahlia, Naked Angels, the Mark Taper Forum, and New Group. His plays have been nominated for the Ovation Award, the Stage Raw Award, the LA Weekly Award, and the GLAAD Media Award.

His writing for TV has been recognized with the Humanitas Prize and the Writer's Guild Award, as well as two Emmy nominations. Along with his writing partner, Jessica Scott, Erik has written films for Warner Bros., Universal, 20th Century Fox, Disney, Freeform, MTV, Paramount, Hallmark, and Syfy, among others. Film and TV credits include: *Abandoned* (starring Emma Roberts and Michael Shannon), *R.L. Stine's The Haunting Hour*, *Another Cinderella Story* (starring Selena Gomez and Jane Lynch), *Deep Blue Sea 2*, *Radio Rebel*, and many more.

Erik is a graduate of Occidental College and the British American Drama Academy. He hosts a gently-guided writing sprint online called "Sunday Sprints" that attracts writers seeking community and inspiration to do their best work.

www.erikpatterson.org

Plays by Erik Patterson

Tonseisha
drama / 1 female, 5 male / 45 minutes, no intermission
A young Japanese woman is haunted by the loss of two men: her father, whom she barely knew, and cult novelist Richard Brautigan, whom she never met. Akiko plays out her father/Richard Brautigan fantasies with a new man nearly every night. Each one of her relationships begins in a bar and ends in a bedroom, and she's never satisfied. She's so lost...can she ever be found?

Yellow Flesh / Alabaster Rose
dark comedy / 5 female, 4 male / full length, one intermission
Elliot is lost in a world of sex workers—late night house calls from hustlers and phone calls with call girls. Becky is torn between two worlds—her day job as a stripper and being a mom to fifteen-year-old Rose (a Goth girl who wants nothing to do with her). And then there's Little B, who has stripped away every piece of herself until all she has left is her obsession with Icelandic pop singer Bjork. This troubled family's shared past holds unspeakable horrors and they must join forces if they ever want to heal. *Winner of the Backstage West Garland Award for Best Playwriting.*

Red Light, Green Light
drama / 6 female, 7 male / full length, one intermission
A gay clown. Two lesbian strippers. A pregnant Goth teen. A deadbeat dad. A horny mother. And a girl who thinks she's Bjork. In this stand-alone sequel to *Yellow Flesh / Alabaster Rose*, the Silverstein family journey towards healing is abruptly halted when Elliot becomes the victim of a brutal gay bashing.

He Asked For It
drama / 1 female, 6 male / full length, one intermission
It's the early 2000s, before PrEP. Ted is new to Los Angeles, and newly out of the closet. He goes on a journey through Hollywood back rooms, nightclub bathrooms, and Internet chat rooms—where he meets and falls in love with Henry. But Henry doesn't yet know how to navigate the dating landscape with his new HIV diagnosis, so he breaks things off with Ted...who then makes a desperate decision to win Henry back. *He Asked For It* asks how far are you willing to go for love? And how much will you forgive? *GLAAD Media Award nominee for Outstanding Los Angeles Theater.*

Sick
dramedy / 3 female, 3 male, 1 child / full length, no intermission
David needs to get laid, Gary could use a drink, and Tim would like you to take your top off. Carla craves cocaine, Jeannie's got God, and Pamela keeps digging herself deeper into the funny and frightening world of hypochondria. But when one of their own gets sick for real, they're all going to have to face their greatest fears and grow up.

I Wanna Hold Your Hand
dramedy / 3 female, 3 male / full length, no intermission
Our lives can change in an instant. One moment you're getting engaged, and a few surreal moments later you're sitting with strangers in an ICU waiting room, praying your fiancé will survive a brain aneurysm. While waiting for Frank to wake from a coma, Ada meets Julia, Paul, and Josh, who are waiting for their mom to wake up. A tenuous friendship is born. *I Wanna Hold Your Hand* looks at life, death, and recovery, and what it means to try your hand at living again...

One of the Nice Ones
dark comedy / 2 female, 2 male / 90 minutes, no intermission
A paraplegic woman plays outrageous power games to get something she desperately wants in this dark, twisty, sexy play that takes office politics to new extremes. *Winner of the Los Angeles Drama Critics Circle Award for Best Playwriting.*

Handjob
dark comedy / 2 female, 4 male / 90 minutes, no intermission
An encounter between a white, gay playwright and his black, straight "shirtless maid" goes disastrously wrong when signals are misinterpreted, lines crossed. *Handjob* explores the aftermath of their meeting, as it reveals deep layers of discrimination, discord, and discontent among people who should be allies. How do you know when you've gone too far if you completely ignore other people's boundaries?

Books by Erik Patterson

Pop Prompts: 200 Writing Prompts Inspired by Popular Music
Available in paperback and e-book

Pop Prompts is a collection of writing prompts that will help you dig deeper and break through creative blocks. Each prompt is paired with a pop song. Let the music be your muse as you work on your memoir, novel, script, poem—or even your own songs. This book can also be a daily jumpstart for therapeutic journaling. Use it however you want, whenever you want. As long as you're writing you're doing it right.

Pop Prompts For Swifties: 99 Writing Prompts
Available in paperback and e-book

Every writing prompt in this book is paired with one of Taylor's songs from the first "era" of her storytelling journey, from her debut album *Taylor Swift* (2006), to *Fearless* (2008), to *Speak Now* (2010), to *Red* (2012), and all the way through *1989* (2014). You don't even have to be a Swiftie—anyone can use these prompts for self-expression and reflection. As a bonus, each prompt includes blank journal pages. Inspiration is only a song away. Put on your favorite Taylor Swift album, pick a prompt, and start writing! Taylor Swift has no involvement in this book. The use of her name is merely descriptive and should not be interpreted as a sign of endorsement.

SUNDAY SPRINTS

Need some motivation?

Do you work better when someone is holding you accountable?

Come to SUNDAY SPRINTS.

Erik Patterson hosts gently-guided writing sprints on Zoom every Wednesday from 6 to 8 p.m. PST and every Sunday from noon to 2 p.m. PST. (Yes, it's called Sunday Sprints on Wednesdays because... why not?)

Here's how it works: I give a new writing prompt every fifteen minutes. You write. That's it.

All sprinters stay on mute. Alone but not alone, you can draw creative energy from the community of writers on your screen. This is a fun, low-pressure environment—a safe space for you to experiment with your writing. No worries: I will never ask you to share your work.

You decide how to use this distraction-free writing time. Work on that screenplay, novel, short story, play, poem, song. Do some therapeutic journaling. Write letters to loved ones. Do some technical writing. Create a D&D campaign. Finish your homework. Seriously, whatever you need to work on.

Let's get that writing done. Together.

Join the Sunday Sprints Patreon at:
www.patreon.com/erikpatterson

Subscribe to the Sunday Sprints mailing list at:
www.erikpatterson.org/sundaysprints

www.ingramcontent.com/pod-product-compliance
Lightning Source LLC
Chambersburg PA
CBHW072058110526
44590CB00018B/3225